COOL FACTS
GOD AND THE BIBLE
kids edition

AUBREY MOORE

ILLUSTRATIONS BY LIL' CRUISERS

Published by:
RipplEffect Books
www.rippleffectbooks.com

First Edition Published 2025
10 9 8 7 6 5 4 3 2 1

Cover Art©: BJO
Interior Design by ©: Aubrey Moore

Scripture References:
Scripture quotations marked NIV are taken from the Holy Bible, New International Version®, NIV®. Copyright © 1973, 1978, 1984, 2011 by Biblica, Inc.™ Used by permission. All rights reserved worldwide. Scripture quotations marked NLT are taken from the Holy Bible, New Living Translation, copyright © 1996, 2004, 2015 by Tyndale House Foundation. Used by permission of Tyndale House Publishers, Carol Stream, Illinois 60188. All rights reserved.

This book is a work of nonfiction. Some stories or examples may have been adapted for clarity and teaching purposes. All Bible facts are presented in a manner suitable for children and grounded in biblical truth.

Printed in the United States of America

Moore, Aubrey
Cool facts God and the Bible / Aubrey Moore
p. cm.
ISBN: 979-8-9875080-2-2

TO MY LITTLE DISCIPLES AND CRUISERS IN TRAINING
KAIYA AND HAYLEE:
I LOVE WATCHING YOU TWO GROW IN YOUR FAITH. I CAN'T
WAIT TO SEE WHAT GOD HAS IN STORE FOR YOU!
LOVE YOU BOTH!
-MAMA

For everyone who asks receives; the one who seeks finds;
and to the one who knocks, the door will be opened.
Matthew 7:8 (NIV)

TABLE OF CONTENTS

SCAN ME!

Cruisers! At the end of each chapter, there's a Bible Study Guide. Scan the QR code and be taken to a special video from the Author for further chapter study and insights!

BONUS! Next to some photos you'll see a QR code - Scan these to see time lapse of the illustrators Haylee (8) and Kaiya (11) drew for this book!

Welcome
to the Cruiser Crew!

Hey there Cruiser! We want to welcome you to the 'Cruiser Crew Family'! What does that mean? It means you cruise with Jesus — and us — the 'Jerusalem Cruisers'! You are now in a group of kids who are brave enough to explore the Bible, ask big questions, and follow Jesus no matter what!
This book was not given to you by accident. We know that God has a special plan for you, and we hope this book helps give you the confidence to become a true disciple of Jesus (don't worry—we'll explain what this means in a little bit).
Do you have a lot of questions about how the universe is made, or how it's possible for God to be with you wherever you go? That's great!
I wrote this book for my daughters, who, like you, have lots of questions about God. A creative and curious mind is a mind that has no limits! You are curious about the world and why things are the way they are, and we're here to help guide you through some of the amazing things God has created for His people!
Are you ready for some fun, cool facts about God you can share with your friends and family? Let's get started!

With Love,

Aubrey Moore AND

1

YOU WILL NEED...

There are a few tools we want you to have with you while you're reading this fun and interactive book:

01
A Bible

If you don't have one, ask an adult if you can borrow theirs! There are tons of online sources, too. With permission from an adult, search: bible.com. We use "NLT and NIV" Bible translations as these are easier to read!

02
Your Journal

You can use a journal, lined paper, or even construction paper! You'll need plenty of paper to take notes and to do your fun activities on. Get creative as you can be with these projects!

03
Your Fav. Pen

Whether it's a gel pen, pencil, or a crayon, it'll work!

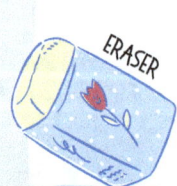

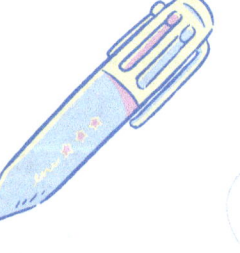

04
An Open Mind and Heart

There are some BIG truths in this book. Some things may sound confusing, but as long as you keep your mind and heart open, the rest will come to light!

LET'S GO!

YOUR FIRST "DID YOU KNOW"!

YAY!

Did You Know God Is Three in One?

It sounds like a mystery—and it is! Not the kind you can't understand. It's more like a "wow!" kind of mystery.

GOD IS...

God the Father (the Creator)

God the Son (Jesus, who came to save us)

God the Holy Spirit (who lives inside believers)

THEY'RE NOT THREE DIFFERENT GODS. THEY ARE ONE GOD IN THREE PERSONS. LIKE A PERFECT **TEAM** WHO ARE ALWAYS IN SYNC—SAME HEART, SAME MISSION, SAME LOVE.

ONE GOD. THREE WAYS HE SHOWS HIS LOVE!

HAVE FAITH

Faith means trusting God—even when you can't see everything.

FAITH FACTS

- FAITH IS HOW WE BELIEVE IN JESUS.
- IT HELPS US KEEP GOING, EVEN ON TOUGH DAYS.
- IT GROWS STRONGER WHEN WE PRAY, READ GOD'S WORD, AND SEE HIM WORK IN OUR LIVES.

"FAITH SHOWS THE REALITY OF WHAT WE HOPE FOR; IT IS THE EVIDENCE OF THINGS WE CANNOT SEE." HEBREWS 11:1 NLT

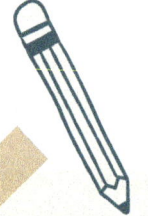

FAITH IN ACTION

Trust God with something small today—like being kind when it's hard. Ask Jesus to help your faith grow a little bigger every day!

Did You Know?

SOME PEOPLE IN THE BIBLE HAD HUGE FAITH—LIKE NOAH, WHO BUILT A GIANT BOAT WITH NO RAIN IN SIGHT... JUST BECAUSE GOD SAID SO! THAT'S SERIOUS TRUST! (GENESIS 6:9–22)

GET TO KNOW YOUR BIBLE

Your Bible is One Big Book Made of 66 Mini-Books!

THERE ARE 2 PARTS TO THE BIBLE

OLD TESTAMANT & NEW TESTAMANT

01. LAW

God's Instructions: 📝
Genesis to Deuteronomy
God's starter rules + how the world began!

02. HISTORY

God's people's adventures: 🏞️
Joshua to Esther
Battles, kings, heroes, and mistakes!

03. POETRY & WISDOM

Full of Songs! 🎶
Job to Song of Solomon
Psalms you can sing + Proverbs to make you wise!

04. PROPHETS

God's Messages: 🔥
Isaiah to Malachi
God sends warnings and promises of Jesus!

01. GOSPELS

Jesus' life: 📖 Matthew to John
The life, love, and miracles of Jesus!

02. THE CHURCH

The Church Begins! 🕊️ Acts
Disciples go out to tell the world!

03. LETTERS

How to Follow Jesus: 🖤
Romans to Jude
Letters full of advice to new believers like YOU!

04. PROPHECY

The Future with Jesus: ☆☆
Revelation
Epic visions of Jesus' return!

HOW TO LOOK UP BIBLE VERSES IN YOUR BIBLE

Example: John 3:16-18 (NLT)
          a.   b.   c.   d.

a. John is the book: go to the book of John
b. 3 is the chapter: find chapter 3 (big number)
c. 16 through 18 is the verse (small numbers)
d. This is the translation of the Bible*

*WE USE NLT & NIV IN THIS BOOK

THE TEN COMMANDMENTS

God gave these important rules to help us love Him and love others!
Think of these as a map throughout your life. If you're not sure if you should do something, ask yourself:
"Does this go against the laws of the Ten Commandments?"

YOU CAN READ ALL ABOUT THESE LAWS IN YOUR BIBLE: EXODUS 20:1—17

COMMANDMENT	WHAT DOES IT MEAN?
"YOU MUST NOT HAVE ANY OTHER GOD BUT ME."	PUT GOD FIRST IN YOUR LIFE — ALWAYS! DON'T TREAT ANYTHING ELSE LIKE IT'S MORE IMPORTANT THAN HIM.
"YOU MUST NOT MAKE FOR YOURSELF AN IDOL OF ANY KIND..."	DON'T WORSHIP STUFF, PEOPLE, OR PRETEND GODS. GOD IS THE ONLY ONE WHO DESERVES OUR WORSHIP.
"YOU MUST NOT MISUSE THE NAME OF THE LORD YOUR GOD."	DON'T USE GOD'S NAME AS A JOKE OR IN A MEAN WAY. HIS NAME IS HOLY!
"REMEMBER TO OBSERVE THE SABBATH DAY BY KEEPING IT HOLY."	REST ONE DAY A WEEK TO SPEND TIME WITH GOD AND YOUR FAMILY — IT'S GOOD FOR YOUR SOUL.
"HONOR YOUR FATHER AND MOTHER."	RESPECT YOUR PARENTS AND LISTEN TO THEM. GOD GAVE THEM TO HELP YOU GROW STRONG AND WISE!
"YOU MUST NOT MURDER."	DON'T HURT OTHERS. GOD WANTS US TO CARE FOR LIFE AND LOVE PEOPLE.
"YOU MUST NOT COMMIT ADULTERY."	BE LOYAL TO YOUR FAMILY AND KEEP YOUR PROMISES, ESPECIALLY IN MARRIAGE.
"YOU MUST NOT STEAL."	DON'T TAKE WHAT ISN'T YOURS — EVEN LITTLE THINGS! BE HONEST AND TRUSTWORTHY.
"YOU MUST NOT TESTIFY FALSELY AGAINST YOUR NEIGHBOR."	DON'T LIE ABOUT OTHERS. ALWAYS TELL THE TRUTH, EVEN WHEN IT'S HARD.
"YOU MUST NOT COVET..."	DON'T BE JEALOUS OF WHAT OTHER PEOPLE HAVE. BE THANKFUL FOR WHAT GOD GAVE YOU!

Did You Know?

GOD GAVE THE TEN COMMANDMENTS TO A MAN NAMED MOSES — ON A REAL MOUNTAIN CALLED MOUNT SINAI! GOD SPOKE OUT LOUD AND EVEN WROTE THE COMMANDMENTS ON STONE TABLETS WITH HIS OWN FINGER! (EXODUS 31:18). THESE WERE GOD'S SPECIAL RULES TO HELP HIS PEOPLE KNOW HOW TO LOVE HIM AND LOVE OTHERS.

WHO IS JESUS?

(and why He is the coolest person ever!)

Jesus is God's Son

He came from Heaven to Earth to show us what God is like — full of love, truth, and power!

He healed the sick, calmed storms, fed huge crowds, and even brought people back to life.

But most of all...

JESUS CAME TO SAVE US.
HE DIED ON A CROSS FOR OUR SINS, ROSE FROM THE DEAD THREE DAYS LATER, AND MADE A WAY FOR US TO BE CLOSE TO GOD FOREVER. JESUS IS THE KING OF KINGS, THE SAVIOR OF THE WORLD, AND YOUR BEST FRIEND EVER.

Jesus is LOVE!

JESUS IS THE GOOD SHEPHERD

Did You Know?

Jesus calls Himself the Good Shepherd — and He knows each of His sheep by name! That means He knows YOU and takes care of you like a shepherd watches over his sheep. He even said and did give His life to protect His sheep — that's how much He loves us! 🤍

"I am the good shepherd. The good shepherd sacrifices his life for the sheep." John 10:11 (NLT)

Did You Know?

In most Bibles, when Jesus is speaking, you'll know because his words will be in RED.

Do This!

Highlight Matthew 28:19 in your Bible as an example!

Did You Know?

Jesus knew people's thoughts without them saying a word! (Luke 5:22)

Did You Know?

Jesus knew the Bible by heart — even as a kid! (Luke 2:46–47)

COOL FACTS

WHOA!

Sheep follow their shepherd's voice — and Jesus said His sheep know His voice too! (John 10:4) In Bible times, shepherds would fight off wild animals to protect their sheep. Jesus fights for you! If one sheep wandered off, a good shepherd would leave the flock to go find it — just like Jesus does for us. (Luke 15:4–6)

FAITH IN ACTION

Follow the Shepherd Challenge

For one whole day, pretend you're a sheep following your Shepherd — Jesus!
Before you make a choice, ask: Would Jesus be proud of this?
Be kind, stay close to what's right, and listen for God's voice (hint: it usually sounds like love, truth, and peace!).

Did You Know?
Jesus fed over 5,000 people with one kid's lunch. (Matthew 14:13–21)

Did You Know?
Jesus walked on water — for real! (Matthew 14:25)

Did You Know?
Jesus calmed a wild storm just by talking to it. (Mark 4:39)

WHO WERE THE DISCIPLES?

THE DISCIPLES WERE JESUS' CLOSEST FOLLOWERS AND FRIENDS.
THEY WEREN'T FAMOUS OR POWERFUL—JUST REGULAR PEOPLE LIKE FISHERMEN AND EVERYDAY WORKERS. JESUS PICKED THEM TO LEARN FROM HIM AND SHARE GOD'S LOVE WITH THE WORLD. THEY FOLLOWED JESUS EVERYWHERE, SAW MIRACLES, AND LEARNED HOW TO LOVE AND SERVE OTHERS. AFTER JESUS ROSE FROM THE DEAD, HE GAVE THEM THE JOB OF SPREADING THE GOOD NEWS TO THE WHOLE WORLD.

"At daybreak He called together all of His disciples and chose twelve of them to be apostles." Luke 6:13 (NLT)

Cool Fact!

SOME OF THE DISCIPLES WERE PROBABLY TEENAGERS OR YOUNG ADULTS WHEN JESUS CALLED THEM!
THAT MEANS YOU'RE NOT TOO YOUNG TO BE PART OF GOD'S BIG STORY.

Big James • John • Thomas • Philip • Bartholomew • Matthew • Thaddaeus • Judas • Little James • Simon Peter • Andrew • Simon the Zealot

THE DISCIPLES HELPED SPREAD THE GOSPEL AROUND THE WORLD
AFTER JESUS ROSE FROM THE DEAD, HIS DISCIPLES TRAVELED TO FARAWAY PLACES TO TELL PEOPLE ABOUT HIM—EVEN WHEN IT WAS HARD OR DANGEROUS. THEY HELPED START THE VERY FIRST CHURCHES!

Kids can be disciples too?! YES! Being a disciple doesn't mean you're perfect—it means you follow Jesus with your heart. You learn what He taught, live how He lived, and help others know Him too.

JESUS GAVE HIS DISCIPLES THE SAME POWER HE HAD!

DID YOU KNOW JESUS GAVE HIS DISCIPLES THE POWER TO HEAL THE SICK, CAST OUT DEMONS, AND PREACH THE GOOD NEWS—JUST LIKE HE DID? HE TRUSTED THEM WITH REAL POWER BECAUSE THEY WERE DOING GOD'S WORK WITH GOD'S HELP. AND GUESS WHAT? HE GIVES YOU THE HOLY SPIRIT SO YOU CAN DO AMAZING THINGS FOR GOD TOO!

JESUS SENT THE DISCIPLES OUT IN PAIRS

JESUS DIDN'T SEND HIS DISCIPLES OUT TO DO THE WORK OF HELPING PEOPLE AND PREACHING THE GOOD NEWS ALONE. HE SENT THEM TWO-BY-TWO SO THEY COULD ENCOURAGE EACH OTHER AND BE STRONG TOGETHER. DISCIPLESHIP IS A TEAM THING! MARK 6:7 (NLT)

WHEN YOU LOOK IN A MIRROR, PICTURE YOURSELF AS JESUS' DISCIPLE!

"One day Jesus called together his twelve disciples and gave them power and authority to cast out all demons and to heal all diseases." Luke 9:1–2 (NLT)

How to Be a Disciple Today:

STEP 1
FOLLOW JESUS STEP-BY-STEP

STEP 2
READ YOUR BIBLE AND LEARN FROM HIM. PRAY TO HIM EVERY DAY

STEP 3
LOVE OTHERS LIKE HE DID

STEP 4
TELL OTHERS WHAT JESUS HAS DONE FOR YOU

Prayer Starter:

"Jesus, I want to follow You like the disciples did. Teach me, lead me, and help me live in a way that shows others who You are. Use me to make a difference—right here, right now. Amen."

PRAY GET CLOSER TO GOD!

"Don't worry about anything; instead, pray about everything."
Philippians 4:6 (NLT)

Did You Know?

YOU CAN TALK TO GOD ANYTIME, ANYWHERE — AND THAT'S CALLED PRAYER!
PRAYER DOESN'T HAVE TO BE FANCY.
YOU DON'T NEED BIG WORDS
JUST TALK TO GOD LIKE YOU WOULD TALK TO A KIND,
LOVING PARENT OR BEST FRIEND.

HOW DO I START PRAYING?

- Talk to God about your day — the good, the bad, and the messy.
- Thank Him for things you're grateful for (like food, friends, pets!).
- Ask Him for help with something you're worried about.
- Say sorry if you did something wrong.
- Just listen. Sometimes prayer means being still and quiet with God.

Did You Know?

The more you pray, the easier it gets — just like learning a new skill.
Prayer can become something you do all the time — while
brushing your teeth, walking the dog, or even before a test!

BECAUSE PRAYER DOESN'T HAVE TO BE BORING!

TRY IT WITH TACOS! ...

T — Thank God for the good stuff in your life.

A — Ask for Help

C — Confess: Tell God anything you did wrong and say sorry.

O — Others First: Pray for someone else — a friend, family member, or even your teacher.

S — Say Anything: God loves when you talk to Him about anything at all!

WHERE CAN I PRAY?

ACTIVITY

Pick a spot in your room or home and get comfy!
Bring your bible, journal, and your favorite pen.
Pray! Use T.A.C.O.S. to help you.
Don't think too much-just start! Let God help you!
Afterward, write in your journal how you feel after praying.

WHAT IF...
I DON'T GET IT?

Confused by what you're reading in the Bible?
That's okay! You're not the only one. Even adults (and pastors!)
sometimes read the Bible and go, "Wait... what does that mean?"
The Bible is a big book full of stories, history, songs, and deep truth. Some
parts are easy to understand—like when Jesus says, "Love your neighbor."
Other parts take time to learn, like a treasure you have to dig for.
God doesn't expect you to understand everything right away. He just wants
you to keep asking, keep learning, and keep talking to Him about it.
That's how we grow!

AND GUESS WHAT? THE HOLY SPIRIT—GOD LIVING INSIDE YOU—HELPS YOU
UNDERSTAND OVER TIME. IT'S LIKE YOU WERE GIVEN SPIRITUAL GLASSES!
SO DON'T GIVE UP. THE MORE YOU READ, THE MORE IT MAKES SENSE. YOU'RE NOT
FAILING—YOU'RE GROWING.

GOD GAVE YOU A NEW WAY
OF LOOKING AT LIFE AND THE
WORLD. IT'S LIKE YOUR OWN
SPECIAL LENS!

Did You Know...

... even Jesus' disciples didn't understand everything at first?

Jesus was patient—and He explained it to them with love!

STORY Time

Jesus taught his followers in what were called **PARABLES** which are basically short, simple stories that helps us learn a big lesson about how to be a good person.

THEN HE OPENED THEIR MINDS TO UNDERSTAND THE SCRIPTURES. — LUKE 24:45 (NLT)

WHEN SOMETHING CONFUSES YOU, TRY THESE IDEAS:

📖 ASK A GROWN-UP WHO FOLLOWS JESUS.

💬 PRAY AND SAY, "GOD, HELP ME UNDERSTAND THIS."

📖 GO TO THE BACK OF THIS BOOK FOR THE GLOSSARY OF COOL WORDS TO HELP YOU!

🔍 LOOK FOR CLUES IN OTHER PARTS OF THE BIBLE.

LET'S START YOUR FAITH JOURNEY!

YOU ARE HERE

YOU JUST STEPPED INTO THE JERUSALEM CRUISERS EXPLORATION ZONE—WHERE WE CRUISE THROUGH ANCIENT LANDS, UNCOVER COOL FACTS, AND DISCOVER HOW GOD SHOWS UP IN REAL PLACES WITH REAL POWER. THE BIBLE ISN'T JUST A BUNCH OF STORIES... IT'S A REAL-LIFE MAP OF WHERE GOD MOVED, HELPED, RESCUED, AND LOVED PEOPLE JUST LIKE YOU. AND GUESS WHAT? YOU GET TO BE PART OF THAT SAME STORY!
LET'S GO CRUISER!

EACH PLACE IN THIS SECTION WILL INCLUDE:

How to Read Your Explorer Guide

Symbol:	What It Means:
Destination	The location we're "cruising" to—like Jericho, the Red Sea, or Bethlehem.
Cool Fact Scroll	A wild, true fact from the Bible that shows off God's awesome power.
Cruiser Gear Tip	A quick lesson for your life—what we can learn from what God did there.
Discipleship Badge	A fun "faith trait" you're building—like obedience, courage, or prayer.
Bible Verse	The real Bible verse where this moment is found. (Yes, it's that legit!)
Action Item	A short activity, challenge, or journal idea so YOU can live out your faith.

Ready to Cruise?

✅ Got your Cruiser gear?
✅ Got your Bible or journal?
✅ Got your Cruiser heart open to what God might want to say?

Let's hit the trail. your first Cruiser Destination starts on the next page!

let's explore the coolest places where heaven touched earth!

CHAPTER 1

CHAPTER THEME: CREATION SHOWS HOW POWERFUL AND REAL GOD IS

Explorer Guide Destination: Jordan River

Cool Fact Scroll:

Did You Know?

God stopped the river's flow so the Israelites could walk into the Promised Land without getting their feet wet!

Cruiser Gear Tip:

God can work miracles all the time, in any situation, and even multiple times! His miracles are endless!

Discipleship Badge: Brave Crosser

Action Item Activity:

Take a small walk outside and imagine the ground you walk on was once a raging river God stopped. Say a thank-you prayer with every step.

Bible Verse:

"As soon as the priests who carried the ark reached the Jordan... the water from upstream stopped flowing." – Joshua 3:15-16 (NIU)

Did You Know God Made Everything?

God had a blank canvas when He created the Universe, much like an artist's canvas!

God made the entire universe out of nothing! He created the sun to shine, the moon to glow, and the stars to sparkle in the sky. He made the oceans deep, the mountains tall, and filled the earth with animals and plants. Every detail, from giant planets to tiny ants, was designed by Him. When we look at creation, we see just how powerful and creative God is! Take a walk outside and observe all the amazing things you see and hear. God's creation is all around you! Let's go through some of these amazing creations together!

Did You Know God Created the Universe With His Voice?
No tools. No machines. Just His powerful words.

MEMORY VERSE

BY THE WORD OF THE LORD THE HEAVENS WERE MADE.

Psalm 33:6 (NIV)

"LET THERE BE LIGHT," AND THERE WAS LIGHT. — GENESIS 1:3 (NIV)

God said it, and BOOM!—the stars, planets, oceans, and animals were all made. Even the weird ones (like the Blobfish)!

The sun is 93 million miles away from the Earth—but God made it in one sentence. How amazing is that?!

"WHOA... THAT'S COOLER THAN MINECRAFT CREATIVE MODE!"

Did You Know God Named Every Star?

Even the tiniest ones you can't see with a telescope.

"HE DETERMINES THE NUMBER OF THE STARS AND CALLS THEM EACH BY NAME." — PSALM 147:4 (NIV)

There are more stars in the sky than grains of sand on Earth—and God knows them all. That means He's pretty good at remembering... which includes remembering you!

WHAT'S THAT MEAN?

IF GOD KNOWS EVERY STAR BY NAME, HE DEFINITELY HASN'T FORGOTTEN YOURS!

SCIENTISTS GUESS THERE ARE OVER 200 BILLION TRILLION STARS. THAT'S A LOT OF NAMES!

Kaiya

Haylee

Callum

JUST LIKE A POTTER MOLDS CLAY GOD MOLDED YOU!

Did You Know God Planned You Before You Were Born?
You're not an accident. You're a masterpiece with a purpose.

"BEFORE I FORMED YOU IN THE WOMB I KNEW YOU." — JEREMIAH 1:5 (NIV)

God thought of you before your parents ever did. He knew your laugh, your smile, your dreams, and even your favorite snack. (Yes, He knew you'd love pizza). Like a clay potter, He molded you just as how He envisioned!

How do you feel knowing that God purposefully made you by His own design? Does this make you look at yourself differently? God hopes so! Every imperfection you think you have, was made by God. How do you think He would feel if He heard you talking bad about yourself? He would probably be very sad. You are His child. He loves you just as you are, just as He designed you, and just as He wants you to be! God says: "You're my idea, and I never mess up!" Now that you know this, share it with someone close to you!

Did You Know Every Living Thing Points Back to a Creator?

Birds know how to fly, bees know how to make honey, and baby animals know how to find their mom. All of that amazing design shows that God is real and very smart!

Did You Know the Bible Gives Evidence That God is Real?

The Bible is full of stories, promises, and prophecies that came true. It's not just a book—it's God's Word, and everything in it points to the truth of who He is.

Did You Know the Universe Follows Rules God Put in Place?

Gravity, seasons, day and night—all of it runs like clockwork. Scientists study those rules, but God made them in the first place!

Did You Know Even Our Brains Are Evidence of God?

Your brain can think, feel, dream, and learn—and scientists still don't understand all of how it works! Something that complex couldn't just happen by chance. God designed every part of you on purpose.

CHAPTER
CHALLENGE

Activity

Let's Make It Stick! Draw something you love about creation— stars, animals, oceans, or YOU! Label it: "God made this!"

TELL SOMEONE
"GOD MADE YOU AWESOME, JUST LIKE THE STARS!"

TALK ABOUT IT
"WHAT'S YOUR FAVORITE THING GOD MADE?"

SHARE
GOD MADE THE WHOLE UNIVERSE, AND STILL HAD TIME TO MAKE YOU AND ME!

COOL
FACT OF THE DAY

IF EARTH WERE JUST A LITTLE CLOSER TO THE SUN, WE'D BURN UP. GOD PLACED IT PERFECTLY!

BIBLE TRUTH FACTS

The Bible is the most-read and most-stolen book in history! It's also the most printed and most translated!

SCAN ME!

YOUR FINGERPRINT IS AS UNIQUE AS YOU

OUT OF THE BILLIONS OF PEOPLE ON EARTH, NO ONE HAS THE SAME FINGERPRINT AS YOU—NOT EVEN IDENTICAL TWINS! AND YOUR FINGERPRINT WAS ALREADY FORMED BY THE TIME YOU WERE JUST A FEW MONTHS OLD IN YOUR MOTHER'S BELLY. THAT MEANS GOD DESIGNED YOU TO BE ONE OF A KIND—ON PURPOSE—AND HE'LL NEVER CONFUSE YOU WITH ANYONE ELSE. HIS LOVE IS PERSONAL, JUST LIKE YOUR FINGERPRINT!

PUT IT IN ACTION

- SOMETHING I WONDER ABOUT GOD....
- I FEEL CLOSE TO GOD WHEN.....
- I'M AMAZED THAT GOD CREATED....
- I WANT TO TELL A FRIEND THIS COOL FACT....
- I WANT TO TELL A FAMILY MEMBER THIS COOL FACT....
- WHAT I WILL START THINKING ABOUT DIFFERENTLY, NOW THAT I KNOW I'M WONDERFULLY MADE....

Grab your journal, or a blank piece of paper and write your answers down! Be sure to share with someone!

PRAY

God, thank You for creating the world—and for making me. Help me always remember You made me special. When I am feeling sad or alone, I pray that I remember you are always with me. Amen.

CHAPTER BIBLE VERSES

Genesis 1:1 (NLT)

"In the beginning God created the heavens and the earth."

Romans 1:20 (NLT)

"For ever since the world was created, people have seen the earth and sky. Through everything God made, they can clearly see his invisible qualities—his eternal power and divine nature. So they have no excuse for not knowing God."

Psalm 19:1 (NLT)

"The heavens proclaim the glory of God. The skies display his craftsmanship."

Colossians 1:16 (NLT)

"For through him God created everything in the heavenly realms and on earth. He made the things we can see and the things we can't see... Everything was created through him and for him."

Isaiah 45:12 (NLT)

"I am the one who made the earth and created people to live on it. With my hands I stretched out the heavens. All the stars are at my command."

Job 12:7–10 (NLT)

"Just ask the animals, and they will teach you. Ask the birds of the sky, and they will tell you. Speak to the earth, and it will instruct you. Let the fish in the sea speak to you. For they all know that my disaster has come from the hand of the Lord. For the life of every living thing is in his hand, and the breath of every human being."

Hebrews 11:3 (NLT)

"By faith we understand that the entire universe was formed at God's command, that what we now see did not come from anything that can be seen."

Nehemiah 9:6 (NLT)

"You alone are the Lord. You made the heavens, even the highest heavens, and all the stars. You made the earth and the seas and everything in them. You preserve them all, and the angels of heaven worship you."

Cruiser Crew Bible Study

 **Recap**

 **SCAN ME!**

AUTHOR INSIGHT

 **Talk About It:**

- **What's the coolest thing you've seen in creation?**
- **Why do you think God made the world so detailed and beautiful?**
- **How does creation remind us that God is powerful?**

 ✅ **Do This!:**

Go outside and find 3 things that show God's creativity (a bug, a cloud, a leaf, etc). Share them with the group and explain how it shows God's power.

✏️ **Journal It:**

Write or draw something amazing God made. Then write: "God, if You can make this, I know You're powerful enough to help me with _____."

 **Bible Goal:**

🌱 **Read Genesis 1 and circle all the things God made that you love most.**

CHAPTER 2

CHAPTER THEME: GOD LOVES DEEPLY, PERSONALLY, and ENDLESSLY

Explorer Guide Destination: Mount Ararat

Cool Fact Scroll:

Did You Know?

After the flood, Noah's Ark came to rest on a real mountain—Mount Ararat. Some people think parts of the Ark might still be up there!

Cruiser Gear Tip:

God's promises land exactly where He says they will.

Discipleship Badge:

Faithful Follower

Action Item Activity:

Build a mini Ark out of paper, cardboard, or Legos. Talk about how God keeps His promises even after the storms.

Bible Verse:

"The ark came to rest on the mountains of Ararat." – Genesis 8:4 (NIV)

Did You Know God Is Crazy About You?

MADE WITH LOVE · MADE WITH LOVE

God's love for you never runs out—it's endless, like the stars in the sky or the waves in the ocean. He doesn't love you because you're perfect; He loves you because you're His. Even when you mess up, He doesn't walk away. His love is strong, constant, and always chasing after your heart. No matter what, God wants you to know this one thing: You are deeply, fully, and forever loved. Even though you can't see Him, God is with you, always. When you are sad, happy, frustrated. He knows your heart, and wants you to know His too!

Did You Know God Knows How Many Hairs are on Your Head?
That's right—every single one!

"EVEN THE HAIRS ON YOUR HEAD ARE ALL NUMBERED." — LUKE 12:7 (NIV)
God doesn't just kinda-sorta love you. He really loves you. So much that He keeps track of stuff no one else could—like how many hairs are on your head. (Even when you get a haircut!)

MEMORY VERSE

"NOTHING CAN SEPARATE US FROM GOD'S LOVE."
Romans 8:39 (NLT)

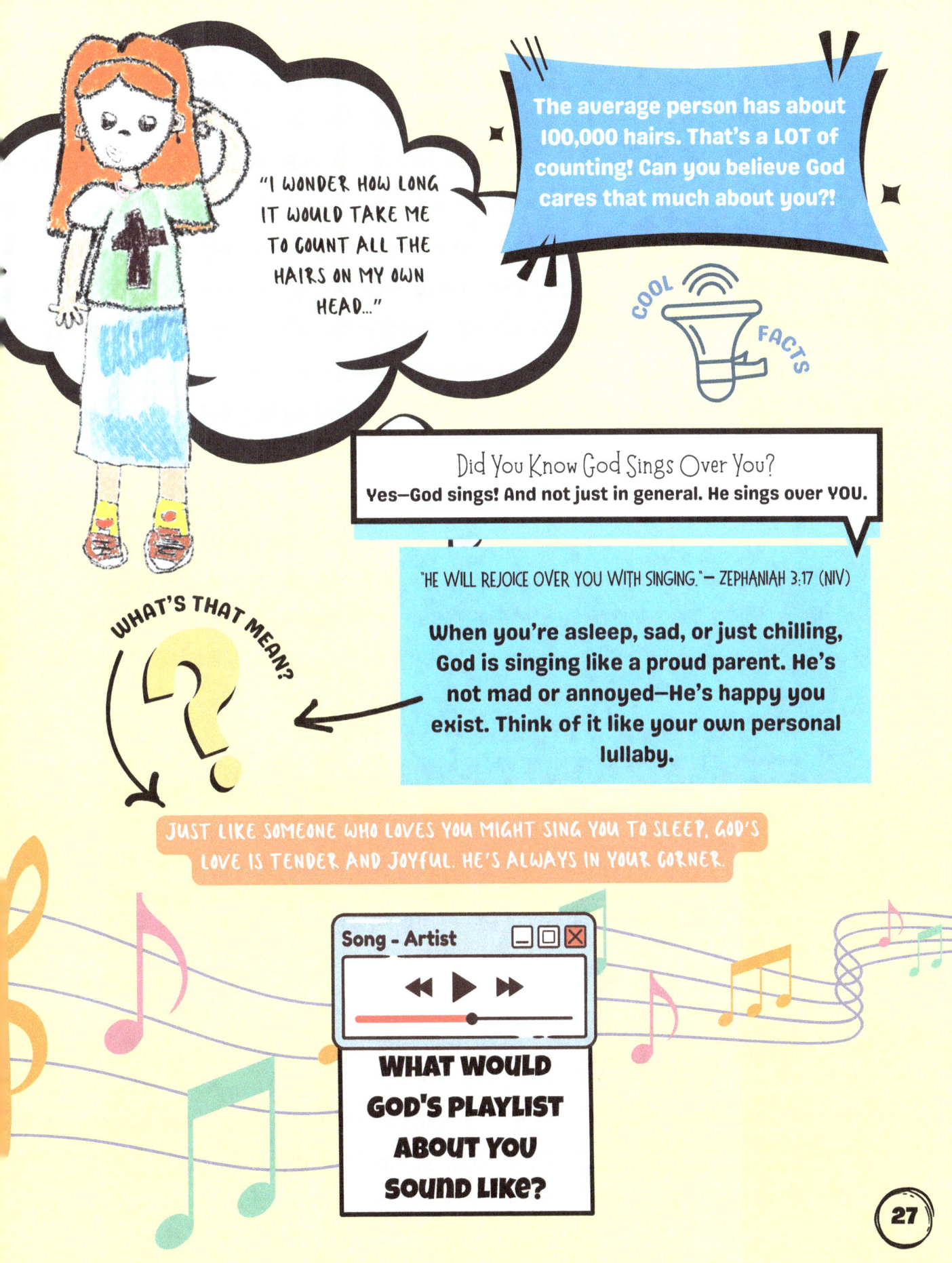

"I WONDER HOW LONG IT WOULD TAKE ME TO COUNT ALL THE HAIRS ON MY OWN HEAD..."

The average person has about 100,000 hairs. That's a LOT of counting! Can you believe God cares that much about you?!

COOL FACTS

Did You Know God Sings Over You?

Yes—God sings! And not just in general. He sings over YOU.

"HE WILL REJOICE OVER YOU WITH SINGING."— ZEPHANIAH 3:17 (NIV)

When you're asleep, sad, or just chilling, God is singing like a proud parent. He's not mad or annoyed—He's happy you exist. Think of it like your own personal lullaby.

WHAT'S THAT MEAN?

JUST LIKE SOMEONE WHO LOVES YOU MIGHT SING YOU TO SLEEP, GOD'S LOVE IS TENDER AND JOYFUL. HE'S ALWAYS IN YOUR CORNER.

Song - Artist

WHAT WOULD GOD'S PLAYLIST ABOUT YOU SOUND LIKE?

BETTER TOGETHER

"NOTHING... CAN SEPARATE US FROM THE LOVE OF GOD." – ROMANS 8:38–39 (NLT)

God's love isn't like a light switch. It doesn't turn off when you mess up or feel far from Him. He loves you forever and always, no matter what!

Think back to a time where you were either really scared (maybe of the dark or a really tall roller coaster). How did you feel in the moment? Most likely you felt alone! Next time you're in a scary moment, think about this: God is with you in that moment! He is your safety net. Whenever you feel all those big feelings, remember, God is right next to you. Much like a safety blanket, he's wrapping you in his arms, singing to you a gentle lullaby, telling you He loves you and to not be scared.

Did You Know God Loves You on Your Best and Worst Days?

God doesn't love you more when you're good or less when you mess up. His love stays the same no matter what. He loves you on your most awesome days—and even when you had a no-good terrible day!

Did You Know God Knows Every Detail About You?

He knows how many hairs are on your head and every thought in your heart. He even knows what you'll say before you say it! God sees it all and still chooses you.

Did You Know You Can Always Rely on Him to be Your Best Friend?

If you're struggling with friends who have hurt you, remember that God is someone you can always talk to. You may not always get a response in the way you want. Just remember, He is always out for your good!

Did You Know God's Love is Bigger Than Anyone Else's?

People might let us down, forget us, or stop loving us—but God never does. His love is higher than the sky and deeper than the sea. Even when others walk away, God stays.

CHAPTER CHALLENGE

Let's Make It Stick!

Activity

Try This!
Write down 3 things you like about how God made you!

TELL SOMEONE
"GOD LOVES YOU LIKE CRAZY!"

TALK ABOUT IT
"WHAT'S ONE WAY YOU KNOW GOD LOVES YOU?"

SHARE
"GOD'S LOVE IS ENDLESS!"

COOL!
FACT OF THE DAY

Your body is about 60% water, and the Earth is over 70% water

CONNECTION TO GOD'S LOVE: THINK ABOUT HOW VITAL WATER IS FOR LIFE. EVERY PLANT, EVERY ANIMAL, AND EVERY HUMAN NEEDS WATER TO SURVIVE AND THRIVE. WATER IS TRADITIONALLY A SYMBOL OF LIFE, PURITY, AND REFRESHMENT. JUST AS WATER SUSTAINS OUR BODIES AND THE EARTH, GOD'S LOVE SUSTAINS OUR SPIRITS. HIS LOVE IS LIKE AN ENDLESS, LIFE-GIVING STREAM THAT NOURISHES US, CLEANSES US, AND HELPS US GROW, JUST AS WATER HELPS A TINY SEED BECOME A MIGHTY TREE. IT'S ALWAYS THERE, ALWAYS FLOWING, ALWAYS GIVING LIFE.

BIBLE TRUTH FACTS

The Bible has over 185 songs written inside it!

Many are in the book of Psalms, but there are also songs sung by Moses, Mary, and even angels!
There are many songs of LOVE for God and God's LOVE for US!

PUT IT IN ACTION

- Write down 3 things you love about yourself. That's how God made you!
- Hug someone and tell them "God loves you!"
- Ask a parent or friend: "What's one way you know God loves you?"

Grab your journal, or a blank piece of paper and write your answers down! Be sure to share with someone!

PRay

Dear God, thank You for loving me all the time—even when I feel unworthy. Help me see myself the way You see me. Show me how to let others know they are loved by you, too! Amen.

CHAPTER BIBLE VERSES

Jeremiah 31:3 (NLT)

"I have loved you, my people, with an everlasting love. With unfailing love I have drawn you to myself."

Romans 5:8 (NLT)

"But God showed his great love for us by sending Christ to die for us while we were still sinners."

1 John 4:9–10 (NLT)

"God showed how much he loved us by sending his one and only Son into the world so that we might have eternal life through him."

Zephaniah 3:17 (NLT)

"For the Lord your God is living among you. He is a mighty savior. He will take delight in you with gladness… He will rejoice over you with joyful songs."

Ephesians 3:18–19 (NLT)

"And may you have the power to understand… how wide, how long, how high, and how deep his love is."

John 3:16 (NLT)

"For this is how God loved the world: He gave his one and only Son, so that everyone who believes in him will not perish but have eternal life."

Psalm 136:1 (NLT)

"Give thanks to the Lord, for he is good! His faithful love endures forever."

1 John 3:1 (NLT)

"See how very much our Father loves us, for he calls us his children, and that is what we are!"

Cruiser Crew Bible Study

Cruiser Check-In: Grow Your Faith Together

 **Recap**

God Loves Deeply, Personally, Endlessly

 **SCAN ME!**

AUTHOR INSIGHT

✅ Do This!:

Make a "God Loves Me" heart poster with your name in the middle. Around it, write or draw ways God shows His love.

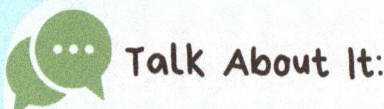 **Talk About It:**

- **What does it mean that God loves you personally?**
- **Have you ever felt like you had to earn love?**
- **How is God's love different from the world's love?**

Journal It:

God, thank You for loving me even when _____.
Help me believe that You'll always love me.
Write 3 more thank you's to God.

1.

2.

3.

Bible Goal:

Replace "everyone" with your name in John 3:16 — then read it out loud as if God is talking straight to you.

CHAPTER 3

CHAPTER THEME: GOD IS ALWAYS WITH YOU—EVEN WHEN YOU FEEL ALONE, SCARED, OR UNSURE.

Scan me!

Explorer Guide Destination: Bethlehem

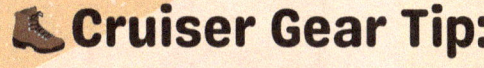

📜 Cool Fact Scroll:

Did You Know?

Jesus, the Savior of the world, was born in a tiny town that most people overlooked.

🥾 Cruiser Gear Tip:

You don't have to be big or important for God to use you in huge ways.

🧢 Discipleship Badge:

Humble Helper

📋 Action Item Activity:

Write a short thank-you letter to Jesus for being born for you—even if you feel small, He sees you as special.

📖 Bible Verse:

"But you, Bethlehem... out of you will come for me one who will be ruler over Israel." – Micah 5:2 (NIV)

Did You Know Jesus is 'God With Us?'

God didn't just make the world and walk away—He's still here, staying close to what He created. From the rising sun to the stars at night, everything keeps working because God is holding it all together. He doesn't forget about the animals, the oceans, or you. Even when people leave or life changes, God stays the same and never walks out on you. The God who made everything is the same God who promises to never leave your side. Think of Him as your best friend. You can talk to him any time you want to, and He is always listening. You can bring all your worries to Him. He wants to help you through anything you have going on in your life.

Did You Know God Is With You All the Time?
That is God's Promise to You!

"BE STRONG AND COURAGEOUS. DO NOT BE AFRAID... FOR THE LORD YOUR GOD IS WITH YOU WHEREVER YOU GO." — JOSHUA 1:9 (NLT)

Whether you're at school, in the car, in your room, or even in the dark, God is right there with you. You don't have to feel Him to know He's close—He promised to never leave. That means you're never really alone.

MEMORY VERSE

"THE WORD BECAME FLESH AND MADE HIS DWELLING AMONG US."

John 1:14 (NIV)

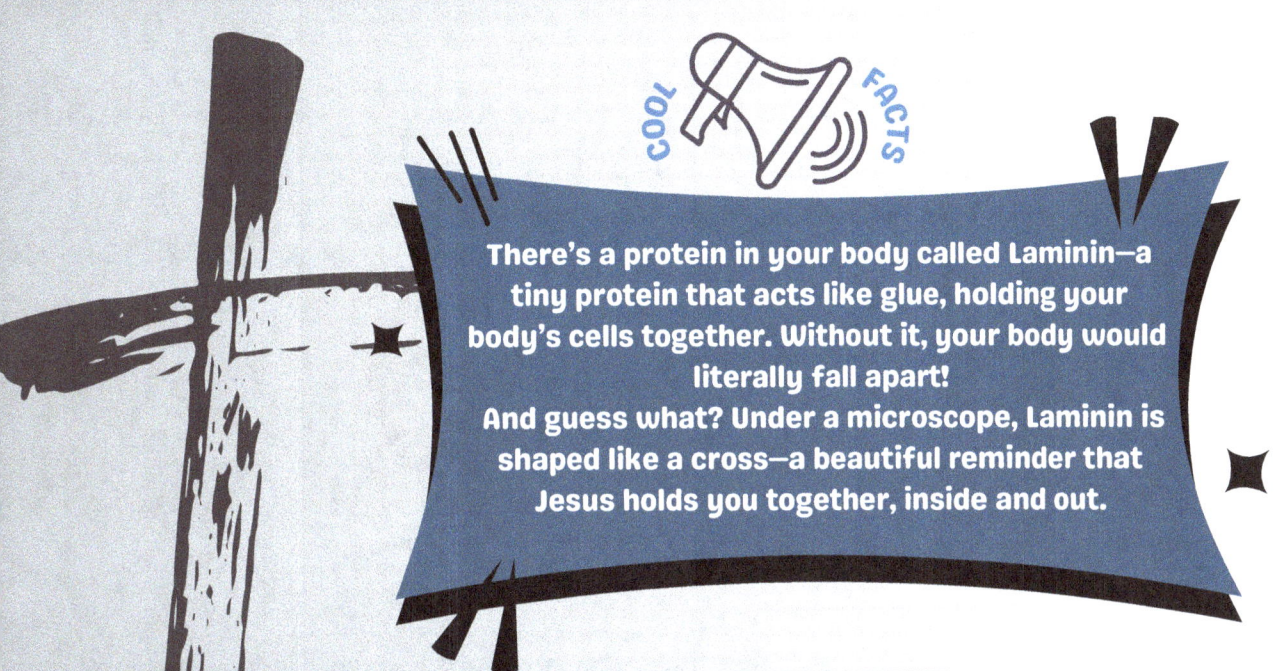

There's a protein in your body called Laminin—a tiny protein that acts like glue, holding your body's cells together. Without it, your body would literally fall apart!
And guess what? Under a microscope, Laminin is shaped like a cross—a beautiful reminder that Jesus holds you together, inside and out.

Did You Know God Stays Close When Life Feels Messy or Hard?

He leaves hints for us all the time that He is near!

"CHRIST... HOLDS ALL CREATION TOGETHER." — COLOSSIANS 1:17 (NLT)

When you feel sad, scared, or like no one understands you—God does. He's near when you're crying and listening when you whisper a prayer. He doesn't leave when life gets tough; He gets closer.

WHAT'S THAT MEAN?

God is Omnipresent. This means: God is not limited by space and time and is present everywhere at once. He is able to be with you and everyone else at the same time - that's some major power!

THERE IS NO HOURGLASS FOR GOD!

Did You Know Jesus Was a Kid Like You?

Yep—Jesus once had sticky hands, stubbed toes, and chores!

AS A BOY, JESUS WORKED WITH HIS FATHER WHO WAS A CARPENTER. THIS WAS LONG BEFORE HE BECAME THE JESUS WHO WORKED MIRACLES!

"JESUS GREW IN WISDOM AND IN STATURE AND IN FAVOR WITH GOD AND ALL THE PEOPLE." — LUKE 2:52 (NLT)

He had a family, celebrated holidays, and probably knew what it felt like to get a splinter. Unlike us, Jesus never sinned— not even once!

Jesus was man and God. That may sound confusing, but everything God does is not by accident! He sent Jesus to Earth to help us understand His love for us never fails, and that we can have eternal life with Him in Heaven! Jesus felt sadness when His friend died. He got tired from walking miles. He was even tempted by Satan—but He never gave in. Jesus was just like us, however, He never sinned. He was the PERFECT savior! Because of Him, we can have eternal life. Be thankful for His sacrifice of his life on the cross, so that we may be forgiven of our sins.

⊕ Did You Know Even When You Walk Away, God Doesn't?

Sometimes we mess up or forget about God. But He never forgets about us. He waits patiently, like a loving Father who's always ready to welcome us back with open arms.

⊕ Did You Know Jesus Described Himself as a Shepherd Who Never Loses His Sheep?

Jesus once told a story about a shepherd who left 99 sheep just to go find the one that was missing. That's how much He cares about you. Even when you feel lost or far away, God comes looking for you.

⊕ Did You Know There's Nowhere You Can Go That's Too Far for God?

Even if you went to outer space or the deepest part of the ocean, God would already be there. The Bible says there's no place where you can hide from His presence. That's how big—and how close—God really is.

⊕ Did You Know God's Presence Isn't Based on How "Good" You Are?

You don't earn God's closeness by being perfect. His love and presence are a gift, not a prize. That means you can talk to Him, feel Him near, and trust that He's with you—even on your messiest days.

CHAPTER CHALLENGE

Let's Make It Stick!

Write or draw one thing Jesus might've done as a kid that you also do.

PRAY

NEXT TIME YOU FEEL LONELY OR HURT, WHISPER: "JESUS GETS IT. HE'S WITH ME."

TALK ABOUT IT

ASK A LOVED ONE: "WHAT DOES IT MEAN TO YOU THAT JESUS IS 'GOD WITH US'?"

SHARE

JESUS WAS FULLY GOD AND FULLY HUMAN—JUST SO HE COULD RESCUE YOU AND ME!

COOL! FACT OF THE DAY

Earth is spinning at over 1,000 miles per hour—and we don't even feel it!

THE EARTH IS MOVING THROUGH SPACE SUPER FAST, SPINNING LIKE A GIANT BALL—BUT EVERYTHING STAYS BALANCED AND STEADY. THAT'S BECAUSE GOD KEEPS IT ALL IN PERFECT ORDER.

JUST LIKE HE KEEPS THE UNIVERSE FROM FLYING APART, HE HOLDS YOUR LIFE TOGETHER TOO. EVEN WHEN THINGS FEEL OUT OF CONTROL, GOD NEVER LETS GO.

BIBLE TRUTH FACTS

There was a boy king in the Bible who became king at just 8 years old!

His name was Josiah (2 Kings 22:1), and he led God's people back to truth at a young age. Even at a young age, Josiah showed a desire to please God. In his eighth year as king, he began seeking God, and in his twelfth year, he started to stop Judah and Jerusalem from <u>idolatry</u> (see glossary).

PUT IT IN ACTION

- **Whisper a Prayer When You Feel Alone**
- **Carry a Reminder of God's Presence:** Make a small "God is with me" card or bracelet to keep in your backpack, pocket, or locker. Every time you see it, remember: You're never alone.
- **Encourage Someone Who Feels Left Out:** Find one person this week who looks lonely or left out—and sit with them, talk to them, or include them. Just like God never leaves you, you can show others that they matter too. This is a great opportunity to talk to them about the love of Jesus!

Grab your journal, or a blank piece of paper and write your answers down! Be sure to share with someone!

PRAY

Dear God, I am so thankful that you are with me all the time, especially when I feel alone. Teach me to live like Jesus, and to love others like you love me. All that you have created is wondrous and beautiful and I am so thankful I get to learn more about you everyday!
Amen.

CHAPTER BIBLE VERSES

Joshua 1:9 (NLT)

"This is my command—be strong and courageous! Do not be afraid or discouraged. For the Lord your God is with you wherever you go."

Deuteronomy 31:6 (NLT)

"So be strong and courageous! Do not be afraid and do not panic before them. For the Lord your God will personally go ahead of you. He will neither fail you nor abandon you."

Isaiah 41:10 (NLT)

"Don't be afraid, for I am with you. Don't be discouraged, for I am your God. I will strengthen you and help you."

Psalm 139:7–10 (NLT)

"I can never escape from your Spirit! I can never get away from your presence... If I go up to heaven, you are there; if I go down to the grave, you are there."

Hebrews 13:5 (NLT)

"For God has said, 'I will never fail you. I will never abandon you.'"

Matthew 28:20 (NLT) (Jesus Speaking)

"And be sure of this: I am with you always, even to the end of the age."

Psalm 23:4 (NLT)

"Even when I walk through the darkest valley, I will not be afraid, for you are close beside me."

Romans 8:38–39 (NLT)

"Nothing can ever separate us from God's love... Neither our fears for today nor our worries about tomorrow... will ever be able to separate us from the love of God."

Cruiser Crew Bible Study

Cruiser Check-In: Grow Your Faith Together

 **Recap**

God Is Always With You—Even When You Feel Alone, Scared, or Unsure

 SCAN ME! **AUTHOR INSIGHT**

 ✅ **Do This!:**

Take turns sharing "scary" or "worry" moments, and then say together: "I am never alone—God is with me!"

💬 **Talk About It:**

- **When have you felt alone or scared?**
- **What helps you remember that God is with you?**
- **How can we help each other trust God in hard times?**

✏️ **Journal It:**

God, today I feel _____, but I know You're still with me. Please remind me that You're close. Write about times you've felt God near you. How did you feel?

 **Bible Goal:**

Memorize Joshua 1:9. Say it every morning before school or when you feel nervous.

CHAPTER 4

CHAPTER THEME: YOU WERE MADE ON PURPOSE, FOR A PURPOSE! GOD DIDN'T JUST CREATE YOU TO EXIST—HE GAVE YOU GIFTS, A CALLING, AND A REASON TO SHINE FOR HIM IN THE WORLD.

Explorer Guide Destination: Mt. Sinai

Cool Fact Scroll:

Did You Know?

God gave Moses the Ten Commandments on a smoky, fiery mountain—complete with thunder and a trumpet sound from the sky!

Cruiser Gear Tip:

When God speaks, even mountains listen. Are you listening too?

Discipleship Badge:

Truth Listener

Bible Verse:

"The Lord descended to the top of Mount Sinai and called Moses to the top of the mountain."
– Exodus 19:20 (NIV)

Action Item Activity:

Write down 3 ways you can follow God's instructions this week. Keep it in a prayer journal and check back each day.

41

Did You Know God Made You for a Purpose?

You're not here by accident—God made you on purpose, with a purpose! He carefully created you with your own personality, gifts, and heart so you can do amazing things for Him. That means even your hobbies, dreams, and kind actions can be part of the good plan He has for your life. No one else can be you, and the world needs what God put inside you. Your purpose starts right now—not someday when you're older.

SCAN ME!

Just like a seed is planted on purpose to grow, so were you!

Did You Know God Picked the Time and Place You'd Be Born?
That is God's Promise to You!

"HIS PURPOSE WAS FOR THE NATIONS TO SEEK AFTER GOD… AND FIND HIM." — ACTS 17:26(NLT)

You weren't born "whenever" or "wherever." God chose this exact moment in history and your exact family on purpose. He placed you here because the world needs you right now!

MEMORY VERSE

"FOR WE ARE GOD'S MASTERPIECE. HE HAS CREATED US ANEW IN CHRIST JESUS, SO WE CAN DO THE GOOD THINGS HE PLANNED FOR US LONG AGO."

Ephesians 2:10 (NLT)

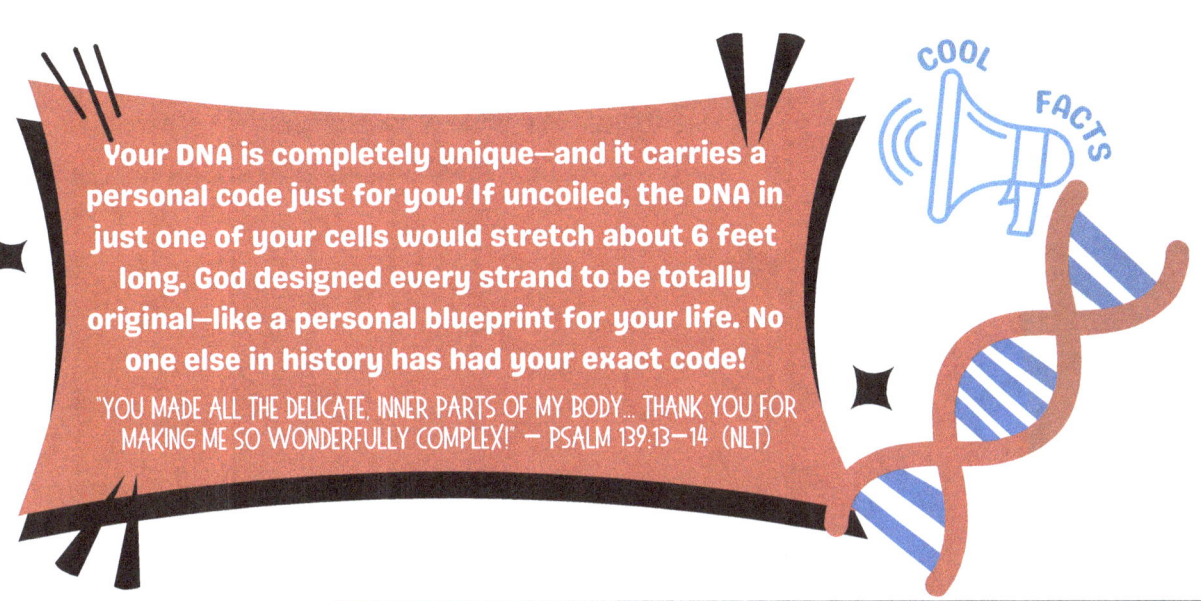

Your DNA is completely unique—and it carries a personal code just for you! If uncoiled, the DNA in just one of your cells would stretch about 6 feet long. God designed every strand to be totally original—like a personal blueprint for your life. No one else in history has had your exact code!

"YOU MADE ALL THE DELICATE, INNER PARTS OF MY BODY... THANK YOU FOR MAKING ME SO WONDERFULLY COMPLEX!" — PSALM 139:13—14 (NLT)

Did You Know You're Not an Accident?
God knew exactly what He was doing when He made you.

WHAT'S THAT MEAN?

"I AM YOUR CREATOR. YOU WERE IN MY CARE EVEN BEFORE YOU WERE BORN." — ISAIAH 44:2 (NLT)

This verse means that God is the one who made you, and He was already loving and caring for you before you were even born. You're not here by accident—God had a plan for your life from the very beginning.

Before you were even born—before your parents even knew you—God already had you in His heart. He was watching over you and forming every part of you with care. You're not here by chance or mistake; God planned your life and gave you special gifts for a reason. That means you matter, and your life has meaning, because the God of the universe personally created you.

Did You Know God Gave You Special Gifts to Use for Good?
He wants you to use your special gifts for others!

"IN HIS GRACE, GOD HAS GIVEN US DIFFERENT GIFTS…"
ROMANS 12:6 (NLT)

Some people are great at encouraging, some love helping, some are brave leaders, and some are quiet and wise. All those gifts come from God—and He gave them to you on purpose.

Some kids are great at leading or speaking, while others are good at listening, serving, or comforting someone who's sad. Whatever your gift is, God wants you to use it for good. That's part of being a <u>disciple</u>, which means being a follower of Jesus who lives like Him, learns from Him, and helps others know Him too. When you use your gifts to love people, stand up for what's right, and serve others, you're living out your purpose as one of Jesus' disciples!

Did You Know You Can Tell Others About God—Even as a Kid?
You don't have to be a grown-up to talk about Jesus. God loves to use kids to shine His light! Your voice matters.

Did You Know God Can Use Even Your Struggles for Good?
Sometimes the hard stuff you go through is part of your story and your purpose. God can turn your pain into power that helps others heal.

Did You Know Even Small Things Matter to God?
Helping someone, saying something kind, or including someone left out may feel small—but God uses those things in BIG ways. Little choices can lead to big change.

Did You Know God Has a Plan Just for You?
Your life isn't random. God has a good plan for you—He's writing a special story that only you can live.

CHAPTER

CHALLENGE

Let's Make It Stick!

Write down what you are really good at (being a good friend, drawing, or maybe singing). Write a thank you card to God thanking Him for your talents!

Do One Thing On Purpose

PICK ONE ACTION TODAY THAT SHOWS GOD'S LOVE—HELPING A SIBLING, ENCOURAGING A FRIEND, OR DOING A CHORE WITHOUT BEING ASKED.

Encourage Another Kid in Their Purpose

TELL A FRIEND SOMETHING GOOD YOU SEE IN THEM. WHEN WE CALL OUT PURPOSE IN OTHERS, WE GROW STRONGER IN OUR OWN!

COOL FACT OF THE DAY

Your brain sends more messages every day than all the phones in the world—combined!

INSIDE YOUR HEAD ARE ABOUT 86 BILLION NEURONS (TINY CELLS THAT SEND SIGNALS). THOSE NEURONS CAN SEND UP TO 1,000 SIGNALS PER SECOND, HELPING YOU THINK, MOVE, FEEL, AND DREAM.

THAT MEANS YOUR BRAIN—DESIGNED BY GOD—IS ONE OF THE MOST POWERFUL SYSTEMS IN THE ENTIRE WORLD! GOD GAVE YOU THAT AMAZING BRAIN TO THINK, CREATE, AND LIVE WITH PURPOSE.

BIBLE TRUTH FACTS

The Bible was written by over 40 authors on 3 continents in 3 languages—but tells one story. It was written in Hebrew, Aramaic, and Greek—on Asia, Africa, and Europe.

PUT IT IN ACTION

- **Purpose Poster:** Draw a poster with your name in the center and words or pictures of what makes you unique around it (your gifts, favorite things, kind actions, etc.). Title it: "God Made Me for a Purpose!"
- **Secret Purpose Mission:** Do one "secret mission" to help someone this week—without telling them. It could be leaving a kind note, helping a sibling, or praying for a friend. Then write about how it felt to do something good just because God made you to be a blessing.

Be sure to share with someone!

PRAY

Dear God, thank you for creating me on purpose. Thank you for all the gifts you have given me, in which I pray I can use to fulfill the plan you have for my life. Open my eyes, my heart, and my mind to the things you want me to do. Thank you that you chose me!
Amen.

CHAPTER BIBLE VERSES

★ HIGHLIGHT THESE IN YOUR BIBLE

Ephesians 2:10 (NLT)

"For we are God's masterpiece. He has created us anew in Christ Jesus, so we can do the good things he planned for us long ago."

Jeremiah 29:11 (NLT)

"For I know the plans I have for you,' says the Lord. 'They are plans for good and not for disaster, to give you a future and a hope."

Psalm 139:13–14 (NLT)

"You made all the delicate, inner parts of my body and knit me together in my mother's womb. Thank you for making me so wonderfully complex! Your workmanship is marvelous—how well I know it."

1 Timothy 4:12 (NLT)

"Don't let anyone think less of you because you are young. Be an example to all believers in what you say, in the way you live, in your love, your faith, and your purity."

Romans 12:6 (NLT)

"In his grace, God has given us different gifts for doing certain things well."

Proverbs 16:9 (NLT)

"We can make our plans, but the Lord determines our steps."

Matthew 5:14–16 (NLT)

"You are the light of the world—like a city on a hilltop that cannot be hidden... Let your good deeds shine out for all to see, so that everyone will praise your heavenly Father."

Isaiah 64:8 (NLT)

"And yet, O Lord, you are our Father. We are the clay, and you are the potter. We all are formed by your hand."

Cruiser Crew Bible Study

Cruiser Check-In: Grow Your Faith Together

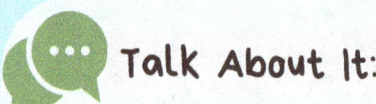 **Recap**

You Were Made On Purpose, For a Purpose!

 **SCAN ME!**

AUTHOR INSIGHT

 ✅ **Do This!:**

Draw yourself in superhero gear, and label your "God-given powers" (kindness, joy, creativity, etc.). Talk about how you can use them for God.

 **Talk About It:**

- **What makes you special or unique?**
- **What are some talents or things you enjoy?**
- **Why do you think God gave you those?**

Journal It:

Pray: "God, thank You for making me special. Help me discover the purpose You've given me." Write positive things about yourself and thank God for each of them!

1.

2.

3.

4.

5.

 **Bible Goal:**

✨**Ask someone you trust (a parent or friend): "What's one gift you see in me that God can use?" Write it down and thank God for it!**

CHAPTER 5

CHAPTER THEME: GOD GIVES US EACH A SPECIAL HELPER, A TRUE POWER INSIDE OF US!

Explorer Guide Destination: The Red Sea

Cool Fact Scroll:

Did You Know?

God split the Red Sea right down the middle so His people could walk across on dry land—with giant walls of water on both sides!

Cruiser Gear Tip:

No road? No problem. God makes paths where there are none.

Discipleship Badge: Waymaker Watcher

Action Item Activity:

Fold a paper in half. On one side, draw something you feel stuck in. On the other, draw where you want to go. Pray in the "middle" space and ask God for help crossing over.

Bible Verse:

"The waters were divided, and the Israelites went through the sea on dry ground." – Exodus 14:21-22 (NIV)

Did You Know God Gives You Superpowers?

Did you know that you don't have to be the loudest, bravest, or strongest person to do amazing things for God? The Holy Spirit is God's invisible helper who lives inside every believer—and He gives you the power to speak up, do what's right, and face hard stuff, even when you're scared. You might feel nervous sometimes, but the Holy Spirit gives you boldness and wisdom in quiet ways. He's like a secret superpower that helps you live with courage, love others well, and make choices that honor God. When you stay connected to Him, you don't have to face anything alone.

Did You Know You Have the Same Power That Raised Jesus?
That's not a Marvel movie—it's real.

"YOU WILL RECEIVE POWER WHEN THE HOLY SPIRIT COMES UPON YOU."
ACTS 1:8 (NLT)

When you follow Jesus, God gives you a special helper—the Holy Spirit. He gives you power to be brave, strong, wise, kind, and full of peace. That's better than x-ray vision! What could you do with that superpower?

MEMORY VERSE

"THE SPIRIT OF GOD, WHO RAISED JESUS FROM THE DEAD, LIVES IN YOU."

Romans 8:11 (NLT)

Did you know that wind is made of moving air particles that can travel at over 100 miles per hour—even though you can't see them? Wind happens when the sun heats up parts of the Earth unevenly, causing warm air to rise and cooler air to rush in and take its place. This invisible movement of air is strong enough to shake trees, power wind turbines, and even create huge storms! Scientists study wind patterns to predict weather, fly airplanes, and design kites and gliders.

Did You Know the Bible Says the Holy Spirit Is Like the Wind?

You can't see it, but you can FEEL it!

"THE WIND BLOWS WHEREVER IT WANTS... SO IT IS WITH EVERYONE BORN OF THE SPIRIT." JOHN 3:8 (NLT)

You can't hold wind in your hands or see it with your eyes, but you can feel it push, hear it blow, and see its power when trees bend or kites fly.

WHAT'S THAT MEAN?

In the Bible, Jesus said the Holy Spirit moves like the wind—you can't see where it comes from or where it's going, but you can feel it. God created the wind, and He uses it as a picture to show us how the Holy Spirit works: powerful, invisible, and always moving with purpose. Just like wind fills a sail and moves a boat, the Holy Spirit fills your heart and helps guide your life.

51

> ## Did You Know God Makes You Brave?
> **Even when you're scared, God gives you strength.**

"GOD HAS NOT GIVEN US A SPIRIT OF FEAR, BUT OF POWER, LOVE AND SELF-CONTROL." — 2 TIMOTHY 1:7 (NIV)

The Holy Spirit helps you speak up, do the right thing, and face hard stuff. You don't need to be loud or tough—just connected to Him.

You know God is with you, always, and now you understand it is the Holy Spirit inside of you that guides your steps and helps you determine right and wrong. You might feel nervous sometimes, but the Holy Spirit gives you boldness and wisdom in quiet ways. He's like a secret superpower that helps you live with courage, love others well, and make choices that honor God. When you stay connected to Him, you don't have to face anything alone.

Did You Know the Holy Spirit Is Called Your Helper in the Bible?
Jesus promised to send the Holy Spirit to be with us all the time—as a helper, guide, and comforter. That means you're never alone when you need to make a hard choice or stand up for what's right.

Did You Know the Holy Spirit Helps You Know What to Say?
When you're not sure how to talk about Jesus or respond to someone, the Holy Spirit gives you the words. Even kids can speak with wisdom and boldness when they listen to His voice!

Did You Know the Holy Spirit Gives You Power to Do Big Things?
The Holy Spirit doesn't make you a superhero, but He gives you courage, kindness, and strength that goes beyond what you can do on your own. He helps you follow Jesus—even when it's hard.

Did You Know You Can Feel the Holy Spirit Leading You?
Sometimes the Holy Spirit speaks through your thoughts, a feeling of peace, or a reminder of a Bible verse. When you pause and listen, you can feel Him guiding you like a gentle whisper inside your heart.

CHAPTER CHALLENGE

Let's Make It Stick!

Write down what you are really good at (being a good friend, drawing, or maybe singing). Write a thank you card to God thanking Him for your talents!

TALK ABOUT IT

TELL SOMEONE ALL ABOUT YOUR SUPERPOWER (THE HOLY SPIRIT) AND LET THEM KNOW THEY CAN HAVE IT INSIDE OF THEM TOO IF THEY JUST BELIEVE!

BE BRAVE

PRAY OUT LOUD IN FRONT OF OTHERS! AND REMEMBER-YOU HAVE THE HOLY SPIRIT INSIDE YOU TO HELP YOU BE BRAVE!

COOL FACT OF THE DAY

Did You Know the Holy Spirit Helps You Grow Fruit?

NOT APPLES AND BANANAS… BUT FRUIT OF THE SPIRIT—GOD'S CHARACTER GROWING INSIDE OF YOU! YOU CAN'T FAKE THIS KIND OF FRUIT. GOD GROWS IT IN YOU WHEN YOU STICK CLOSE TO HIM. WHAT'S THAT MEAN? IT'S LIKE YOUR SPIRITUAL POWER-UP! PEOPLE SEE JESUS IN YOU WHEN THEY SEE YOUR FRUIT.

"THE FRUIT OF THE SPIRIT IS LOVE, JOY, PEACE, PATIENCE, KINDNESS, GOODNESS, FAITHFULNESS, GENTLENESS, AND SELF-CONTROL." — GALATIANS 5:22-23 (NIV)

BIBLE TRUTH FACTS

The Bible Is the Best-Selling Book of All Time! Over 5 billion copies have been sold or given away—and it's been translated into more than 3,500 languages! No other book even comes close. That's because the Bible isn't just a book—it's God's message to the whole world.

PUT IT IN ACTION

Listen First Challenge

- Each morning this week, take one quiet minute to pray: "Holy Spirit, help me hear You today. Show me how to do the right thing and love like Jesus."
- Then—pay attention! Maybe you'll feel a nudge to help a classmate, say something kind, or stand up for someone.

Be sure to share with someone!

PRAY

Holy Spirit, thank You for living in me. Help me be brave, kind, and full of truth. Lead me every day to do what's right, even when it's hard. I want to follow You! Amen.

CHAPTER BIBLE VERSES

⭐ HIGHLIGHT THESE IN YOUR BIBLE

Acts 1:8 (NLT)

"But you will receive power when the Holy Spirit comes upon you. And you will be my witnesses, telling people about me everywhere…"

John 14:26 (NLT)

"But when the Father sends the Advocate as my representative—that is, the Holy Spirit—he will teach you everything and will remind you of everything I have told you."

Galatians 5:22–23 (NLT)

"But the Holy Spirit produces this kind of fruit in our lives: love, joy, peace, patience, kindness, goodness, faithfulness, gentleness, and self-control…"

Romans 8:14 (NLT)

"For all who are led by the Spirit of God are children of God."

2 Timothy 1:7 (NLT)

"For God has not given us a spirit of fear and timidity, but of power, love, and self-discipline."

Isaiah 11:2 (NLT)

"And the Spirit of the Lord will rest on him—the Spirit of wisdom and understanding, the Spirit of counsel and might, the Spirit of knowledge and the fear of the Lord."

Romans 8:26 (NLT)

"And the Holy Spirit helps us in our weakness. For example, when we don't know what God wants us to pray for, the Holy Spirit prays for us with groanings that cannot be expressed in words."

Luke 12:12 (NLT)

"For the Holy Spirit will teach you at that time what needs to be said."

Cruiser Crew Bible Study

Cruiser Check-In: Grow Your Faith Together

God Gives Us Each a Special Helper, a True Power Inside Us!

AUTHOR INSIGHT

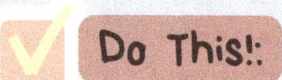 **Do This!:**

Hold your hand over your heart and say: "God's Spirit is with me. I can be bold, kind, and wise!"

Talk About It:

- **Who is the Holy Spirit?**
- **What does the Holy Spirit help us do?**
- **Have you ever felt God help you do something hard or kind?**

Journal It:

Holy Spirit, help me today when I feel _____. I want to listen to You.

Write 3 other ways you'd like the Holy Spirit to help you throughout your day.

1.

2.

3.

 **Bible Goal:**

Read John 14:26 and write next to this verse in your Bible: "Holy Spirit" so you always remember who the "helper" is.

CHAPTER 6

CHAPTER THEME: God is Real, and He gives us the power to stand up for our beliefs!

Explorer Guide Destination: JERICHO

Cool Fact Scroll:

Did You Know?

The walls of Jericho came crashing down because God's people obeyed His wild instructions—marching, shouting, and blowing trumpets!

Cruiser Gear Tip:

Obedience might not always make sense, but it makes miracles happen.

Discipleship Badge: Obedience Explorer

Action Item Activity:

Draw a "wall" on paper, write fears or struggles on the bricks, then pray and crumple it as a sign of trusting God to knock them down.

Bible Verse:

"By faith the walls of Jericho fell, after the army had marched around them for seven days." – Hebrews 11:30 (NIV)

Did You Know You Can Defend Your Faith?

The Bible says to always be ready to give an answer about your hope in Jesus, and the Holy Spirit helps you do that with kindness and courage. When you know who God is and how real His love is, you can help others see the truth about Him too. You don't have to be a Bible expert—you just have to trust that God will help you speak when it matters most.

Did You Know You Honor God by Saying YES to Him?

God isn't just an "idea"—He's the real Creator of the universe!

"SINCE THE CREATION OF THE WORLD GOD'S INVISIBLE QUALITIES... HAVE BEEN CLEARLY SEEN." ROMANS 1:20 (NIV)

You don't have to be afraid when people say God isn't real. Look at nature. Look at your own heart. Everything points to Him. Start with understanding that God created the universe. Let others know this truth too!

MEMORY VERSE

"ALWAYS BE READY TO GIVE AN ANSWER... FOR THE HOPE THAT YOU HAVE. BUT DO THIS WITH GENTLENESS AND RESPECT."
1 Peter 3:15 (NIV)

Did you know that your bones are about five times stronger than concrete of the same size? Even though bones are lightweight and hollow in some places, God designed them to handle tons of pressure and still stay strong. That's kind of like your faith—it may not always look big or loud, but with God, it's built to stand strong under pressure. Just like bones grow stronger when you use them, your faith grows when you speak it, defend it, and trust God—no matter what.

Did You Know the Bible is 100% True?
It's not a fairytale—it's God's Word.

WHAT'S THAT MEAN?

"EVERY WORD OF GOD PROVES TRUE. HE IS A SHIELD TO ALL WHO COME TO HIM FOR PROTECTION." — PROVERBS 30:5 (NLT)

When someone questions the Bible, don't panic. Ask questions, stay kind, and dig deeper!

The Bible isn't a made-up story or a book full of pretend people—it's real history! Archaeologists (people who dig up ancient things) have found cities, coins, scrolls, and even royal seals that match what the Bible says. Scientists and historians continue to discover evidence that proves the people, places, and events in the Bible really existed. Best of all, the Bible doesn't just tell us what was true—it tells us what's true for our lives right now. Everything God says in His Word can be trusted—because it really happened and it's still changing lives today.

WALLS OF JERICHO

"GOD HAS NOT GIVEN US A SPIRIT OF FEAR, BUT OF POWER, LOVE AND
SELF-CONTROL." — 2 TIMOTHY 1:7 (NIV)

**Real Discovery: The Walls of Jericho –
They Really Fell Down!**

The Bible says in Joshua 6 that the walls of the city of Jericho came crashing down after the Israelites marched around them and shouted—just like God told them to. Some people thought that sounded too wild to be true... But guess what? Archaeologists discovered the ancient city of Jericho, and they found that the walls really did collapse outward—just like the Bible says! That's super rare, because walls usually fall inward when a city is attacked. This shows that God's power is real—and the Bible's history can be trusted.

Did You Know You Can Stand Up for Jesus Without Being Mean?

God doesn't want us to win arguments—He wants us to love people well.

Did You Know Archaeologists Have Found Over 25,000 Bible-Related Sites and Artifacts?

From ancient scrolls to buried cities and battlefields, real discoveries keep proving the Bible is based on true events. The more scientists dig, the more the Bible's history is confirmed!

Did You Know Even One Kid Who Believes Can Make a Big Difference?

In the Bible and in real life, God has used kids and young people to lead, speak up, and stand out. When you boldly say, "I believe in Jesus," you're being a brave defender of the truth—just like a spiritual superhero.

Did You Know God Keeps Every Promise—and That's Why You Can Trust Him?

Defending your faith starts with knowing that God never breaks His word. The more you learn what the Bible says, the stronger your faith becomes—and the more confidence you'll have to speak up when others doubt Him.

CHAPTER
CHALLENGE

Let's Make It Stick!

Write down one thing you'd say to someone if they asked you: "Why do you believe in God?"

Talk About It:

ASK AN ADULT: "HOW DO YOU EXPLAIN YOUR FAITH WHEN OTHERS QUESTION IT?"

Role Play with a Friend or Parent

ASK SOMEONE YOU TRUST TO PRETEND TO BE CURIOUS OR CONFUSED ABOUT GOD. PRACTICE EXPLAINING WHO JESUS IS AND WHY YOU BELIEVE IN HIM. YOU DON'T NEED PERFECT WORDS—JUST BE HONEST AND LET YOUR LOVE FOR JESUS SHINE!

COOL
FACT OF THE DAY

Gravity Never Changes (Just Like God's Truth!)

DID YOU KNOW THAT GRAVITY ALWAYS WORKS THE SAME, NO MATTER WHERE YOU ARE ON EARTH? WHETHER YOU'RE JUMPING IN TEXAS OR CLIMBING A MOUNTAIN IN AFRICA, GRAVITY PULLS YOU DOWN AT THE EXACT SAME FORCE—EVERY SINGLE TIME. SCIENTISTS TRUST IT SO MUCH, THEY USE IT TO LAUNCH ROCKETS, BUILD SKYSCRAPERS, AND DESIGN AIRPLANES. WHY? BECAUSE TRUTH DOESN'T CHANGE—AND THAT'S EXACTLY HOW GOD'S WORD WORKS TOO. GOD'S TRUTH IS SOLID AND DEPENDABLE, AND IT ALWAYS HOLDS YOU UP, EVEN WHEN LIFE GETS SHAKY.

PSALM 119:89 (NLT) — "YOUR ETERNAL WORD, O LORD, STANDS FIRM IN HEAVEN."

BIBLE TRUTH FACTS

The Bible was written over 1,500 years by 40+ authors—yet it tells one story: how much God loves us. History, prophecy, science, and archaeology back it up!

PUT IT IN ACTION

- **Build Your Faith Talk Card**
  - Grab an index card or a small piece of paper and create your own "Why I Believe" card. On one side, write or draw:
    - One reason you believe in God
    - One thing you know is true about Jesus
    - A favorite Bible verse you'd share with a friend
  - On the back, write a prayer asking God to help you speak with love and courage when someone asks you about your faith.

  Be sure to share with someone!

PRAY

Dear God, help me be bold and kind when I talk about You. Help me love people while standing strong in what I believe. Let your words, not my own, speak to those that are doubting you, through me.
Amen.

CHAPTER BIBLE VERSES

⭐ HIGHLIGHT THESE IN YOUR BIBLE

Psalm 119:160 (NLT)

"The very essence of your words is truth; all your just regulations will stand forever."

2 Corinthians 10:5 (NLT)

"We destroy every proud obstacle that keeps people from knowing God. We capture their rebellious thoughts and teach them to obey Christ."

Hebrews 4:12 (NLT)

"For the word of God is alive and powerful. It is sharper than the sharpest two-edged sword..."

Psalm 18:30 (NLT)

"God's way is perfect. All the Lord's promises prove true. He is a shield for all who look to him for protection."

James 1:22 (NLT)

"But don't just listen to God's word. You must do what it says. Otherwise, you are only fooling yourselves."

Titus 1:9 (NLT)

"He must have a strong belief in the trustworthy message he was taught; then he will be able to encourage others with wholesome teaching and show those who oppose it where they are wrong."

Isaiah 55:11 (NLT)

"It is the same with my word. I send it out, and it always produces fruit. It will accomplish all I want it to..."

Matthew 10:32 (NLT)

"Everyone who acknowledges me publicly here on earth, I will also acknowledge before my Father in heaven."

Cruiser Crew Bible Study

Cruiser Check-In: Grow Your Faith Together

 **Recap**

God Is Real, and He Gives Us the Power to Stand Up for Our Beliefs!

SCAN ME!

AUTHOR INSIGHT

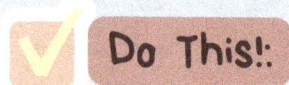 ☑️ **Do This!:**

Role-play a moment when someone questions your faith. Practice answering with truth and kindness.

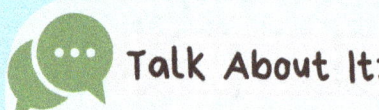 **Talk About It:**

- **What do you believe about God?**
- **Has it ever been hard to say you're a Christian?**
- **How can you stand strong when others don't believe?**

Journal It:

Jesus, help me stand strong in my faith—even when it's hard. I want to be brave for You. Write down a time(s) you felt scared or nervous to talk about God with others. What is something you could do to help you be more confident next time?

 **Bible Goal:**

Find one Bible verse about standing strong (like Ephesians 6:10). Write it on a sticky note and put it on your wall or notebook.

CHAPTER 7

CHAPTER THEME: GOD TURNS BAD THINGS INTO GOOD!

📜 Cool Fact Scroll:

Did You Know?

Jesus knew one of his disciples would betray Him, but He still chose to love him.

🥾 Cruiser Gear Tip:

When life feels hard, don't run away—pray like Jesus did.

🧢 Discipleship Badge: Courageous Pray-er

📋 Action Item Activity:

Find a quiet place. Talk to God about something hard you're going through. Write your prayer in a journal or whisper it out loud.

📕 Bible Verse:

"Being in anguish, He prayed more earnestly, and His sweat was like drops of blood falling to the ground."
– Luke 22:44 (NIV)

Did You Know God Understands Your Struggles?

SCAN ME!

Because Jesus lived as a human. He totally gets what you're going through—whether you're hurt, stressed, left out, or confused. The amazing part? He doesn't leave you in your struggle. He promises to walk with you, help you, and give you strength when life gets tough. You don't have to hide your hard days from Him—Jesus understands and stays right by your side.

Did You Know the Shortest Bible Verse in the Bible is:
"Jesus wept." John 11:35 NLT

Did You Know Jesus Went Through Really Hard Things?
Jesus lived the perfect life, but not without trials, including being crucified on a cross and losing his life.

"THIS HIGH PRIEST OF OURS UNDERSTANDS OUR WEAKNESSES, FOR HE FACED ALL OF THE SAME TESTINGS WE DO, YET HE DID NOT SIN." HEBREWS 4:15 (NLT)

JESUS FELT ALL THE FEELINGS WE FEEL, INCLUDING BEING SCARED! HE HAD FRIENDS, LOST LOVED ONES, AND HELPED CARE FOR PEOPLE HE DIDN'T EVEN KNOW. HE DIED FOR YOU, FOR US, FOR EVERYONE! THAT'S PRETTY AMAZING. WHAT'S IMPORTANT TO KNOW IS, JESUS DID ALL OF THIS SO THAT WE HAVE THE OPPORTUNITY TO LIVE ETERNITY WITH HIM AND GOD IN HEAVEN!

MEMORY VERSE

"THE LORD IS CLOSE TO THE BROKENHEARTED AND SAVES THOSE WHO ARE CRUSHED IN SPIRIT."
Psalm 34:18 (NIV)

Did You Know Diamonds Are Made Under Pressure?
Diamonds are one of the hardest and most beautiful things on Earth—but they start as plain, black carbon buried deep underground. It takes extreme pressure and heat over a long time to turn that ordinary carbon into a sparkling diamond! That's kind of like what God does with our struggles. He doesn't waste pain, sadness, or confusion—He uses it to shape us into something stronger, wiser, and more beautiful. Just like carbon can become a diamond, God can turn your hard moments into something that shines for His glory.

Did You Know God Can Turn Bad Things Into Good?
Even when things feel messed up, God is working behind the scenes.

"IN ALL THINGS GOD WORKS FOR THE GOOD OF THOSE WHO LOVE HIM." — ROMANS 8:28 (NIV)

That doesn't mean everything feels good— but it means nothing is wasted. God uses hard stuff to grow us stronger, kinder, and closer to Him.

WHAT'S THAT MEAN?

Sometimes bad things happen—things that hurt, don't make sense, or feel totally unfair. It's important to know that God doesn't cause those bad things, but He can still use them to do something amazing in your life. Think of it like a puzzle—when you only see one piece, it might not look good at all. God sees the whole picture, and He can take even the broken pieces and turn them into something beautiful. Even when life gets topsy-turvy, God is working behind the scenes to grow your heart stronger, build your faith, and show you His love in deeper ways.

Did You Know Jesus Was Tempted by Satan for 40 Days in the Desert?
Jesus Never Gave Into the Devil!

"THEN JESUS WAS LED BY THE SPIRIT INTO THE WILDERNESS TO BE TEMPTED THERE BY THE DEVIL." MATTHEW 4:1 (NLT)

The desert where Jesus was tempted is real! It's called the Judean Desert, and it's a hot, rocky, dry place with barely any food or water—a tough place to be for 40 days.

After Jesus was baptized, He went into the wilderness and didn't eat for 40 days! During that time, Satan tried to trick Him into doing wrong—but Jesus never gave in. Even though He was tired and hungry, Jesus stayed strong by using God's Word. Jesus prayed, a lot, and let God know his struggles. Jesus knows what it's like to be tempted, tired, and even hungry—but He never sinned, not even once. That means He understands how hard it can be when you're trying to do the right thing. When you're feeling pressured to make a wrong choice, Jesus gets it—and He's ready to help you stand strong too. Just like Jesus used Bible verses to fight back, you can remember God's truth to help you make good choices, even when it's tough. You're not alone—Jesus has been there, and He's with you now.

Did You Know Jesus Cried?
When His friend Lazarus died, Jesus wept just like you might when you're sad (John 11:35). That shows His heart is full of love—and He understands your pain too.

Did You Know Paul Wrote Parts of the Bible From Prison?
Even in chains, Paul shared hope, joy, and truth with the early church. God used a hard time to write words that still encourage us today!

Did You Know Jesus Calmed a Storm Just by Speaking?
One time, His disciples were terrified in a wild storm—and Jesus told the wind and waves to stop... and they did! He can bring peace to your stormy days, too. (Mark 4:39)

Did You Know Three Guys in the Bible Survived a Fiery Furnace?
Shadrach, Meshach, and Abednego stood up for God—and He protected them in the fire. When you stand strong, God stands with you. (Daniel 3)

CHAPTER
CHALLENGE

Let's Make It Stick!

What is a lie you've told yourself (for example: "I'm not good enough," "I'm always alone," "I can't do something."

Now write down the opposite: "I AM good enough. God is ALWAYS with me. I CAN do this.

Talk About It:

TELL SOMEONE ABOUT HOW JESUS CRIED, JUST LIKE US.
ASK THEM HOW THAT MAKES THEM FEEL.

Read and Think

READ MATTHEW 4:1-11 AND READ HOW THE DEVIL TEMPTED JESUS. WRITE DOWN, OR TALK TO SOMEONE ABOUT IT AND BE TRUTHFUL: COULD YOU DO THE SAME AS JESUS?

COOL! FACT OF THE DAY

Caterpillars Completely Melt Before Becoming Butterflies!

DID YOU KNOW THAT WHEN A CATERPILLAR GOES INTO ITS COCOON, IT ACTUALLY TURNS INTO LIQUID BEFORE BECOMING A BUTTERFLY? INSIDE THE CHRYSALIS, THE CATERPILLAR DOESN'T JUST GROW WINGS—IT COMPLETELY BREAKS DOWN INTO GOO AND STARTS OVER. THAT MIGHT SOUND WEIRD, BUT IT'S PART OF GOD'S AMAZING DESIGN. EVEN THOUGH THE CATERPILLAR GOES THROUGH A MESSY, HIDDEN PROCESS, SOMETHING BEAUTIFUL IS HAPPENING. JUST LIKE THAT, GOD CAN USE THE MESSY, HARD, OR CONFUSING TIMES IN YOUR LIFE TO SHAPE SOMETHING BRAND NEW AND FULL OF PURPOSE.

2 CORINTHIANS 5:17 (NLT) — "ANYONE WHO BELONGS TO CHRIST HAS BECOME A NEW PERSON. THE OLD LIFE IS GONE; A NEW LIFE HAS BEGUN!"

BIBLE TRUTH FACTS

The Bible has over 300 prophecies about Jesus—fulfilled perfectly (meaning they all actually happened)! These were written hundreds of years before Jesus was born, and every one came true.

PUT IT IN ACTION

- **My Hard Thing Journal Page**
  - Grab a piece of paper or a journal and write down:
    - One hard thing you're going through (big or small)
    - One thing you want God to do in your heart during this time
    - One Bible verse from this chapter that reminds you He's with you
  - You can decorate your page with colors or doodles that show how you feel—because God cares about every part of your story.

    Be sure to share with someone!

PRAY

Dear God, I want to transform, like a butterfly, through the struggles I go through. Thank you for giving us your son, to die for me. I want to prove to you that I can be like Jesus. Please keep me focused to do this everyday!
Amen.

CHAPTER BIBLE VERSES

⭐ HIGHLIGHT THESE IN YOUR BIBLE

James 1:12 (NLT)

"God blesses those who patiently endure testing and temptation... they will receive the crown of life."

2 Corinthians 4:17 (NLT)

"For our present troubles are small and won't last very long. Yet they produce for us a glory that vastly outweighs them and will last forever!"

1 Peter 5:10 (NLT)

"In his kindness God called you to share in his eternal glory by means of Christ Jesus. So after you have suffered a little while, he will restore, support, and strengthen you."

Isaiah 43:2 (NLT)

"When you go through deep waters, I will be with you. When you go through rivers of difficulty, you will not drown."

John 16:33 (NLT) (Jesus Speaking)

"Here on earth you will have many trials and sorrows. But take heart, because I have overcome the world."

Psalm 56:8 (NLT)

"You keep track of all my sorrows. You have collected all my tears in your bottle. You have recorded each one in your book."

Romans 5:3-4 (NLT)

"We can rejoice, too, when we run into problems and trials, for we know that they help us develop endurance. And endurance develops strength of character..."

Psalm 34:18 (NLT)

"The Lord is close to the brokenhearted; he rescues those whose spirits are crushed."

Cruiser Crew Bible Study

Cruiser Check-In: Grow Your Faith Together

 **Recap**

SCAN ME!

AUTHOR INSIGHT

 **Talk About It:**

- Have you ever seen something bad turn into something good?
- How does it feel to know God can use hard things for a purpose?
- Why is it hard to trust God during bad times?

 **Bible Goal:**

Think of a time something hard happened. Tell God about it, then ask Him to help you trust Him with it now.

 ✅ **Do This!:**

Make a "God Can Use This" collage using pictures or words that show tough situations (like a broken toy, a storm) and write how God can still work through it.

Journal It:

God, I don't always understand why hard things happen, but I trust You to use it for good. Write down a time where you went through something hard. What are ways you can ask God for help through those hard times?

CHAPTER 8

CHAPTER THEME: You might feel small sometimes, but your faith is big in God's hands.

Cool Fact Scroll:

Did You Know?

In John 6, a boy offered Jesus five loaves of bread and two small fish. That's it. Jesus turned that small meal into a miracle—feeding thousands with leftovers to spare! That's the power of offering your "small" to a big God.

He Is Risen!

Cruiser Gear Tip:

God's strength shows up when even when you feel weak. Pray before doing something hard and God will protect you!

Discipleship Badge: Faith Builder

Action Item Activity:

Small acts, big impact: for the next 7 days write down something you do each day to serve others. At the end of the week, you'll see how BIG of a difference you made with those small acts!

Bible Verse:

"God chose things the world considers foolish in order to shame those who think they are wise. And He chose things that are powerless to shame those who are powerful." – I Corinthians 1:27 (NLT)

Did You Know Your Faith Can Change the World?

When you follow Jesus and live like Him, you're doing something called being a disciple. That just means you learn from Jesus and help others know Him too. You don't have to be a grown-up or a Bible expert—God uses kids all the time to do big things. When you love like Jesus, stand up for what's right, pray for others, and share your story, you're changing the world.

Did You Know Jesus Picked Regular People as His Disciples?

Jesus didn't choose kings or famous people—He picked fishermen, tax collectors, and young people to follow Him. That means He can use you too!

"ONE DAY AS JESUS WAS WALKING ALONG THE SHORE OF THE SEA OF GALILEE, HE SAW SIMON AND HIS BROTHER ANDREW THROWING A NET INTO THE WATER, FOR THEY FISHED FOR A LIVING. JESUS CALLED OUT TO THEM, 'COME, FOLLOW ME, AND I WILL SHOW YOU HOW TO FISH FOR PEOPLE!'"
MARK 1:16–17 (NLT)

God doesn't look for the fanciest people—He looks for willing hearts. He wants people who will trust Him, learn from Him, and help others know Him. Just like Simon and Andrew, God invites you to follow Him, too. You don't need to be perfect or famous. You just need to say yes to Jesus—and He'll use your life in ways you never imagined.

MEMORY VERSE

"WHOEVER WANTS TO BE MY DISCIPLE MUST DENY THEMSELVES AND TAKE UP THEIR CROSS AND FOLLOW ME."
Matthew 16:24 (NLT)

Did you know that sound can travel over 700 miles per hour? And with the right equipment, even a tiny whisper can be recorded and broadcast around the globe in just seconds! That means one small voice has the power to reach millions of people. That's just like your faith. You might feel small, but when you speak about Jesus or live like Him, God can use your life to spread His love farther than you can imagine. Your voice matters. Your kindness echoes. And your story—no matter how simple—can help change someone else's forever.

Did You Know the Mustard Seed is one of the Tiniest Seeds...
But can grow into a large, strong tree?!

WHAT'S THAT MEAN?

"IF YOU HAD FAITH EVEN AS SMALL AS A MUSTARD SEED... NOTHING WOULD BE IMPOSSIBLE." MATTHEW 17:20 (NLT)

Jesus used the mustard seed as a powerful example in the Bible. He said that even if your faith is as small as a mustard seed, God can still do BIG things with it.

YOU CAN MOVE MOUNTAINS!

The Mustard seed is only about 1 to 2 millimeters wide! That's smaller than a sprinkle on your cupcake! When it's planted and taken care of, it grows into a giant bush or tree, sometimes over 10 feet tall—big enough for birds to land in its branches! That means even if you feel unsure, nervous, or not "good enough," God isn't asking for perfect faith—just real faith. When you trust Him, even in little ways, He grows that faith into something strong, bold, and world-changing. Tiny faith + big God = unstoppable power.

Did You Know David Was Just a Kid When He Beat a Giant?
Ever heard of the Giant named Goliath? No myths here!

SCAN ME!

"DAVID REPLIED... 'YOU COME TO ME WITH SWORD, SPEAR, AND JAVELIN, BUT I COME TO YOU IN THE NAME OF THE LORD OF HEAVEN'S ARMIES.'"
1 SAMUEL 17:45 (NLT)

David wasn't a soldier—he was a young shepherd boy who delivered snacks to his older brothers at war.

When David saw a giant named Goliath mocking God, David stood up with just a slingshot and big faith. Everyone else was scared, but David trusted God to help him. And God did! With one stone, David defeated the giant and showed the whole army what fearless faith can do. The coolest part? David grew up to be King of Israel!

Did You Know? David Wrote Songs (Psalms) to God That Are Still in the Bible Today? Many of the Psalms in the Bible were written by David as prayers and worship songs. Some were written when he was happy, others when he was scared or sorry—but he always talked to God with an honest heart.

⊕ **Did You Know You Can Be a Leader Even If You're Young? (Like David!)**
The Bible is full of young people God used to lead others—He cares more about your heart than your age.

⊕ **Did You Know You're Called to Be a Light?**
When you follow Jesus, your words and actions shine bright in a dark world (Matthew 5:14).

⊕ **Did You Know Faith Is Like a Shield?**
Ephesians 6 says faith protects you—it helps you stand strong when life feels hard or confusing.

⊕ **Did You Know The Disciples Helped Spread Jesus' Message Across the World?**
They started small, but their bold faith helped millions of people know about Jesus.

CHAPTER CHALLENGE

What are ways you can become a disciple of Jesus? Write down 3 things you can start doing today that will honor God. They don't have to be as big as 'David and Goliath'...but then again—why not YOU?!

Talk About It:

ASK SOMEONE YOUNGER THAN YOU HOW THEY FEEL ABOUT BEING "SMALLER" THAN YOU AND TELL THEM: 'EVEN THOUGH YOU'RE SMALLER, IT DOESN'T MEAN YOU AREN'T POWERFUL ENOUGH TO FIGHT A GIANT!'

Share!

TELL SOMEONE ABOUT THE STORY OF DAVID AND GOLIATH AND BE SURE TO TELL THEM IT REALLY HAPPENED!

COOL FACT OF THE DAY

Ants Can Lift 50 Times Their Own Body Weight!

DID YOU KNOW AN ANT CAN CARRY THINGS 50 TIMES HEAVIER THAN ITSELF? THAT WOULD BE LIKE YOU LIFTING A CAR! ANTS ARE TINY, BUT THEY'RE INCREDIBLY STRONG, DETERMINED, AND WORK TOGETHER TO BUILD GIANT COLONIES THAT CAN SURVIVE FOR YEARS.

THAT'S HOW YOUR FAITH WORKS TOO. EVEN IF YOU FEEL SMALL, YOUR TRUST IN GOD IS POWERFUL. WHEN YOU FOLLOW JESUS AND LIVE OUT YOUR FAITH, GOD CAN DO THINGS THROUGH YOU THAT SEEM IMPOSSIBLE—JUST LIKE THE ANT LIFTING SOMETHING HUGE.

PHILIPPIANS 4:13 (NLT) — "FOR I CAN DO EVERYTHING THROUGH CHRIST, WHO GIVES ME STRENGTH."

The Dead Sea Scrolls Match the Bible: In 1947, ancient scrolls were found in caves near the Dead Sea—including pieces of the Old Testament that are thousands of years old and nearly identical to today's Bible. That shows how accurately it's been preserved!

PUT IT IN ACTION

- **Send a Message of Hope**
  - Write a note, draw a picture, or send a message to someone who might need encouragement.
  - Tell them God loves them—and so do you.
  - Being a disciple means sharing God's love in real ways, even through simple acts of kindness.

Be sure to share with someone!

PRAY

Dear God, I want to follow You, not just with my words, but with my whole life. Show me how to live like You, love like You, and tell others about You. Use my faith to help change the world—one step at a time.

Amen.

CHAPTER BIBLE VERSES

Matthew 28:19–20 (NLT)

"Therefore, go and make disciples of all the nations, baptizing them... teaching them to obey everything I have commanded you."

1 Timothy 4:12 (NLT)

"Don't let anyone look down on you because you are young, but set an example for the believers in speech, life, love, faith, and purity."

Matthew 5:16 (NLT)

"Let your light shine before others, so they will see the good you do and praise your Father in heaven."

Acts 1:8 (NLT)

"But you will receive power when the Holy Spirit comes upon you. And you will be my witnesses... to the ends of the earth."

Philippians 2:15 (NLT)

"Live clean, innocent lives as children of God, shining like bright lights in a world full of crooked and perverse people."

Romans 10:14 (NLT)

"How can they call on him to save them unless they believe in him? And how can they believe in him if they have never heard about him?"

Proverbs 11:30 (NLT)

"The seeds of good deeds become a tree of life; a wise person wins friends."

2 Timothy 1:7 (NLT)

"For God has not given us a spirit of fear and timidity, but of power, love, and self-discipline."

Cruiser Crew Bible Study

Cruiser Check-In: Grow Your Faith Together

 **Recap**

You Might Feel Small Sometimes, But Your Faith Is Big in God's Hands

 **SCAN ME!**

AUTHOR INSIGHT

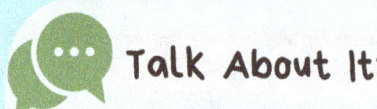 **Talk About It:**

- Have you ever felt too small to make a difference?
- What does the Bible say about small faith (like a mustard seed)?
- How can you be a light in your school, home, or neighborhood?

 ✅ **Do This!:**

Pass around a tiny mustard seed or a small object. Say: "Even this small seed can grow. My faith can grow too!"

Journal It:

God, I may be young, but I believe in You. Use my faith to do something big for You! Write down 3 ideas you can start doing now to help you become a Disciple of Jesus! Remember, nothing is too big or too small for Him!

1.

2.

3.

 **Bible Goal:**

Find a mustard seed verse (like Matthew 17:20). Draw a tiny seed next to it in your Bible or journal. Pray: "God, grow my faith today!"

WHAT NOW?

1 TALK TO GOD EVERY DAY

HE'S NOT TOO BUSY FOR YOU. YOU DON'T NEED FANCY WORDS. JUST TALK LIKE YOU'RE TALKING TO YOUR BEST FRIEND.
TRY THIS: "GOD, THANKS FOR BEING AMAZING. HELP ME TRUST YOU MORE. AMEN!"

2 READ THE BIBLE

PICK A VERSE A DAY. YOU COULD START IN THE BOOK OF JOHN OR PROVERBS. ASK AN ADULT TO HELP YOU FIND A BIBLE THAT'S EASY TO READ.

3 ASK QUESTIONS

IT'S OKAY TO WONDER THINGS LIKE: "WHY DID GOD DO THAT?" OR "WHAT DOES THIS VERSE MEAN?" KEEP ASKING. THAT'S HOW YOU GROW IN FAITH!

4 TELL SOMEONE

TELL A FRIEND, YOUR PARENT, OR SOMEONE NEW YOU MEET, A COOL FACT ABOUT GOD YOU READ IN THIS BOOK. YOU MIGHT HELP THEM BELIEVE, TOO!

5 WHAT IT MEANS

BEING A FOLLOWER OF JESUS ISN'T JUST ABOUT KNOWING THINGS ABOUT HIM—IT'S ABOUT CHOOSING TO LOVE AND FOLLOW JESUS WITH YOUR WHOLE HEART. THAT'S A BIG DECISION, BUT YOU'RE NEVER TOO YOUNG TO ASK QUESTIONS!

Now it's time to take the next steps in your faith journey...

but first you need to know

WHAT IS HEAVEN?

HEAVEN IS... God's forever home—a real place filled with joy, love, and God's presence. It's where there's no more pain, sadness, or sickness. Everyone who believes in Jesus gets to live with Him there forever. It's not floating on clouds or becoming angels—it's better than that! The Bible says Heaven is more amazing than anything we've ever seen or imagined:

NO EYE HAS SEEN, NO EAR HAS HEARD, AND NO MIND HAS IMAGINED WHAT GOD HAS PREPARED FOR THOSE WHO LOVE HIM. – 1 CORINTHIANS 2:9 NLT

1 Did You Know?

Heaven is more beautiful than your wildest dreams! It has streets made of gold, gates of pearls, and a place where no one cries or gets hurt.

And the best part? God is there. Jesus is there. And they want YOU there too.

Believe in the Lord Jesus, and you will be saved." – Acts 16:31 NLT

DID YOU KNOW?

You can't earn your way to Heaven by being good. That's right! Heaven isn't like a prize you win for doing chores, getting straight A's, or being the nicest kid in school. The Bible says that we all mess up sometimes (Romans 3:23), and no matter how "good" we try to be, we could never be perfect enough for God's standard. But here's the BEST news ever:

Jesus already paid the price for you!

READY TO GIVE JESUS YOUR WHOLE HEART AND PROMISE TO FOLLOW HIM ALWAYS?

PRAY

Dear Jesus,

I know I'm not perfect. I've made mistakes and haven't always done the right thing.

Thank You for loving me anyway.

I believe You are God's Son, and You died for my sins.

Please forgive me, come into my heart,

and help me live for You every day.

I want to follow You and be with You forever in Heaven.

Amen!

You must love the LORD your God with all your heart, all your soul, and all your mind.
Matthew 22:37
NLT

fill your daily SCHEDULE with Jesus

HOW?

Jesus says this is the most important thing you can do every day:
Love God with ALL of who you are. Not just on Sundays. Not just when you feel like it. Every day. All day.
But how do you do that?

START HERE

Check Your Time! How do you spend most of your day? If you're spending way more time on video games, scrolling, or watching TV than with God, it might be time to shift things. Loving God more than the world means choosing Him first.

DON'T STOP

Remember, every day, you have the opportunity to spend time with God.
How will you spend your free time? What changes can you make in your schedule?

ACTIVITY

Create your own schedule (or use the one on the next page). Ask a family member to help you. You can even make this a family activity. Every day you can ask each other: "Did you follow your Daily Jesus Schedule?"

Jesus in My
Daily Schedule

Morning – Start with God

- Wake up + stretch
- Read one Bible verse (try Proverbs or Psalms!)
- Say a short prayer: "God, help me live for You today."
- 🎵 Listen to a worship song while you brush your teeth!

During School or Activities

- Be kind. Be honest. Be helpful.
- Whisper a quick prayer if you feel nervous or tempted.
- Think: "What would Jesus do right now?"

Afternoon / After School

- Finish homework → then take 10 minutes with God!
- Read a short Bible story
- Write down 1 thing you learned
- Talk to God about your day

Free Time

- Set a time limit for screens / games
- Try something new:
- Write a verse on a sticky note
- Write a note to a friend of something encouraging
- Draw a picture of a Bible story you love

Evening / Before Bed

- Read one verse (or let a parent read it to you!)
- Thank God for the day
- Ask Him to help you grow in love, kindness, and boldness

CUSTOMIZE YOUR OWN UNIQUE SCHEDULE!
and share with others!

WHAT IS BAPTISM?

Have you heard people talk about being baptized?

> Baptism is when someone is immersed (all-in!) in water to show everyone that they've chosen to follow Jesus. It's kind of like a big announcement: "HEY WORLD! I CRUISE WITH JESUS!"

BECAUSE JESUS TOLD US TO! EVEN JESUS GOT BAPTIZED!

THAT MEANS YOU ARE INVITED TO KNOW HIM AND FOLLOW HIM, NO MATTER HOW YOUNG YOU ARE. JESUS WANTS YOU TO DRAW CLOSE TO HIM!

"LET THE CHILDREN COME TO ME." —MATTHEW 19:14 (NLT)

AM I READY?

Talk with your parent, pastor, or church youth leader if you're thinking about getting baptized. They'll help you know when you're ready.

HOW OLD DO YOU HAVE TO BE?

There's no exact age. You just need to:
- Understand what baptism means
- Believe in Jesus
- Be ready to live for Him

– GLOSSARY –
COOL WORDS TO KNOW
(YOUR GUIDE TO BIG BIBLE WORDS MADE SIMPLE!)

WORD	DEFINTION
God	The one true Creator of everything—He made the world, He loves you, and He's always with you.
Worship	Showing God love and honor through singing, praying, obeying, and living for Him.
Jesus	God's Son who came to earth, lived a perfect life, died for our sins, and came back to life—He's our Savior!
Holy Spirit	God's invisible helper who lives in every believer's heart and helps us follow Jesus.
Sin	Anything we think, say, or do that goes against God's way. It separates us from God—but Jesus forgives us!
Pray / Prayer	Talking to God—just like a conversation! You can pray anytime, anywhere, about anything.
Bible	God's true Word—full of stories, wisdom, and truth to help us know Him better.
Disciple	Someone who follows Jesus, learns from Him, and tells others about Him. (That can be you!)
Baptism	A special way to show others that you've decided to follow Jesus—it's like going public with your faith.
Faith	Believing in God and trusting Him, even when you can't see everything clearly.
Truth	Something that is 100% real and right—God's Word is full of truth!
Grace	A gift from God—His kindness and forgiveness, even when we don't deserve it.
Church	Not just a building! It's God's family—people who believe in Jesus and gather to grow and worship.
Kingdom of God	God's rule and reign—where His love, peace, and power are in charge! We're part of it when we follow Him.
Gospel	The "Good News" that Jesus died for our sins, came back to life, and made a way for us to be close to God forever.
Idolatry	When someone loves or puts something more important than God—like money, stuff, people, or even themselves. God wants to be first in our hearts!

CONGRATULATIONS CRUISER!

Welcome (officially) to the Cruiser Crew! You've learned cool facts about God and the bible... now it's time to go on a real adventure with Him!

BEING A JERUSALEM CRUISER MEANS YOU'RE ON A MISSION TO FOLLOW JESUS EVERYWHERE YOU GO! YOU CAN DO BIG THINGS FOR GOD, EVEN WHILE YOU'RE A KID.

Checklist:
- ✓ I learned cool facts about God
- ✓ I know how to pray
- ✓ I know how to use my Bible
- ✓ I'm ready to live for Jesus!

I CRUISE WITH JESUS

DESIGN YOUR OWN CRUISER DISCIPLESHIP GEAR

DRAW AND COLOR YOUR OWN CRUISER T-SHIRT DESIGN
JUST FOLLOW THE DIRECTIONS BELOW!

SCAN ME!

VISIT: WWW.JCRUISERS.COM/BOOKS

PURCHASE YOUR T-SHIRT
WE'LL EMAIL YOU THE DOWNLOADABLE BLANK T-SHIRT (FRONT AND BACK)
DESIGN YOUR SHIRT, SEND TO US, AND WE'LL SEND YOU YOUR
PERSONALIZED T-SHIRT

20% PROCEEDS ARE DONATED TO NON-PROFITS
FIGHTING HUMAN TRAFFICKING

YOUR EMAIL WILL HAVE DIRECTIONS/NEXT STEPS FOR SENDING US YOUR T-SHIRT DESIGNS

TAG US ON SOCIALS WEARING YOUR WORSHIP
WEAR WITH YOUR COOL FACTS BOOK & WE'LL
SEND YOU A SPECIAL GIFT

ALL SOCIALS: @cruisenarrow

CRUISE narrow

MEET THE CRUISER FAMILY

Haylee · Aubrey · Kaiya · Chris

DO YOU cruise?

About Us

We started Jerusalem Cruisers to help us be more comfortable talking to others about Jesus! We created some shirts with bible verses and cool sayings, and want to help others disciple too! Dada Cruiser Chris, came up with the name: 'Jerusalem Cruisers'!

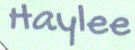

Haylee — 8 yrs old
Future Artist

Haylee loves Jesus, her family, and friends! She wants others to know Jesus loves them too!

<u>Haylee drew art on pages:</u>
Dedication Pg, 4, 6, 12, 22, 27, 30 34-36, 42, 50-51, 58, 60, 62, 66, 70, 73-74, 76, 81, 86, 90

Kaiya — 11 yrs old
Future Astronaut

Kaiya loves to disciple at her church and learn about Jesus and the Bible! She's not afraid to ask questions & find the answers!

<u>Kaiya drew art on pages:</u>
8, 10-11, 15, 20, 33, 38, 44, 68

FOLLOW THE AUTHOR:
@aubreymoorebooks

Grandma BJO — Artist

Cruiser Family Cool Fact:
Kaiya & Haylee's Gma Bonnie painted the cover artwork! Bonnie is Aubrey's mom!

Aubrey Moore — Author

I give God all the honor and glory in my love to write! Since I was 10, I would fill notebooks of stories from dreams I had. I love writing mostly fiction novels, but God put it on my heart to write a children's book. My girls & mom helped me with the artwork and some of the questions too! I want all children to know: Jesus loves YOU!

Follow Us on Social Media

Let's Get Connected for Our Latest News, Updates, and MORE Book Release Dates!

CONNECT WITH US

www.jcruisers.com
info@jcruisers.com

@cruisenarrow

FOLLOW US FOR MORE COOL FACTS BOOKS COMING SOON!

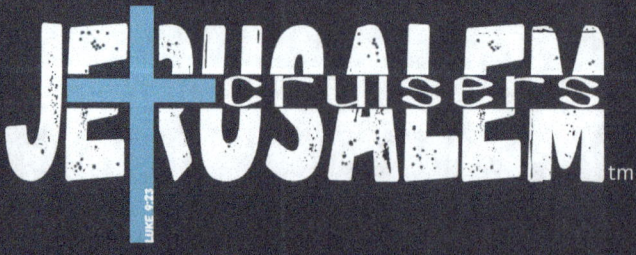